THE HAMLYN LECTURES
FIFTEENTH SERIES

CRIME AND THE

CRIMINAL LAW

AUSTRALIA
The Law Book Company Ltd.
Sydney : Melbourne : Brisbane

CANADA AND U.S.A.
The Carswell Company Ltd.
Agincourt, Ontario

INDIA
N. M. Tripathi Private Ltd.
Bombay
and
Eastern Law House Private Ltd.
Calcutta
M.P.P. House
Bangalore

ISRAEL
Steimatzky's Agency Ltd.
Jerusalem : Tel Aviv : Haifa

MALAYSIA : SINGAPORE : BRUNEI
Malayan Law Journal (Pte.) Ltd.
Singapore

NEW ZEALAND
Sweet & Maxwell (N.Z.) Ltd.
Auckland

PAKISTAN
Pakistan Law House
Karachi

CRIME AND THE
CRIMINAL LAW:

Reflections of a Magistrate and Social Scientist

BY

BARBARA WOOTTON

SECOND EDITION

Published under the auspices of
THE HAMLYN TRUST

LONDON
STEVEN & SONS
1981

First Published — 1963
Second Edition — 1981

Published in 1981 by
Stevens & Sons Limited of
11 New Fetter Lane, London
Printed in Great Britain by
Thomson Litho Limited
East Kilbride, Scotland

British Library Cataloguing in Publication Data

Wootton, Barbara
  Crime and the criminal law. — 2nd ed. — (The
Hamlyn lectures)
  1. Crime and criminals — England — Sociological aspects
  2. Punishment — England — Sociological aspects
  I. Title   II. Series
  364'.942   HV6947

  ISBN 0-420-46170-1
  ISBN 0-420-46180-9 Pbk.

CONTENTS

THE HAMLYN LECTURES

THE HAMLYN TRUST

THE Hamlyn Trust came into existence under the will of the late Miss Emma Warburton Hamlyn, of Torquay, who died in 1941 at the age of eighty. She came of an old and well-known Devon family. Her father, William Bussell Hamlyn, practised in Torquay as a solicitor for many years. She was a woman of strong character, intelligent and cultured, well versed in literature, music and art, and a lover of her country. She inherited a taste for law and studied the subject. She also travelled frequently to the Continent and about the Mediterranean, and gathered impressions of comparative jurisprudence and ethnology.

Miss Hamlyn bequeathed the residue of her estate in terms which were thought vague. The matter was taken to the Chancery Division of the High Court, which on November 29, 1948, approved a Scheme for the administration of the Trust. Paragraph 3 of the Scheme is as follows:

> "The object of the charity is the furtherance by lectures otherwise among the Common People of the United Kingdom of Great Britain and Northern Ireland of the knowledge of the Comparative Jurisprudence and the Ethnology of the chief European countries including the United Kingdom, and the circumstances of the growth of such jurisprudence to the intent that the Common People of the United Kingdom may realise the privileges which in law and custom they enjoy in comparison with other European Peoples and realising and appreciating such privileges may recognise the responsibilities and obligations attaching to them."

The Trustees are to include the Vice-Chancellor of the University of Exeter and representatives of the Universities of London, Leeds, Glasgow, Belfast and Wales. So far as practicable one of the Trustees is to be a person who was under the age of 40 at the time of appointment.

INTRODUCTION

It is not an easy task, in an area where change is as rapid as in criminal law and practice, to update discourses which are already 17 years old. I can but hope that the procedure which I have adopted will be acceptable to readers. I have made as few changes as possible in the original text, but, after consultation with the publishers, have generally modernised terminology, for example, substituting "The Crown Court" for "Quarter Sessions," "Court of Appeal" for "Court of Criminal Appeal" and "theft" for "larceny." Most of the statistics, for example those relating to the volume of crime, remain as printed in the original lectures; but corresponding figures for more recent dates are included in the Postscripts to each chapter, which also record relevant new developments in crime and criminal law, together with some after-thoughts of my own. After much reflection, it seemed to me that it would be more appropriate to attach such new material in each case to the chapter to which it related, rather than to write what would amount to a single additional chapter, covering the whole ground, which would only be intelligible in the light of constant reference back to the relevant lecture.

Apart from these technical details, my task would have been incomparably more burdensome had it not been for the generosity of Messrs. George Allen & Unwin who gave me permission to incorporate verbatim in this revision of my Hamlyn lectures sundry passages from my book on *Crime and Penal Policy* which they published in 1978. Incidentally, readers may like to know that they will find in that book (now paperbacked) much fuller treatment of many of the topics discussed in this new edition of the lectures. For my part I am most happy to use this intro-duction as an opportunity to express to Messrs. Allen & Unwin my deeply felt appreciation of an exceptionally helpful concession which greatly exceeded anything for which I had hoped.

Barbara Wootton

House of Lords
January 1981

Chapter 1

A MAGISTRATE IN SEARCH OF THE CAUSES OF CRIMES

As the only layman who has yet given the Hamlyn lectures, I cannot but be both dazzled by the eminence of the distinguished lawyers who have preceded me and deeply sensible of the honour paid to me by the Trustees. I can only hope that the occasional choice of a layman, and particularly of a specimen of that peculiarly English genus, the lay magistrate, might have appealed to the Founder of this Trust. For Emma Hamlyn's objective, you may remember, was that the common people of this country should realise the privileges which they enjoy in law and custom, and should recognise the responsibilities and obligations attaching to them; and these are certainly matters which are constantly brought to the notice of magistrates and of the common people with whom they have to deal. At all events let me say at once that the reflections on crime and the criminal law which I propose to offer to you are the product of a dual experience extending over more than 30 years—experience, that is to say, on the one hand as a magistrate, and on the other hand as a professional social scientist.

The social scientist who finds himself on the Bench can hardly fail to be sadly impressed by the scale and persistence of criminal behaviour; and by the gross failure of our society to eradicate this. Year by year the criminal statistics record a persistent upward trend in the number of persons convicted of offences in England and Wales, up to a total of 1,152,000 in 1961. In the past ten years such convictions, though actually fewer in 1951 than before the war, have increased by nearly 60 per cent.[1] If, moreover, attention is confined to indictable offences (which are generally, though not in every instance correctly, regarded as the more serious crimes), the increase is more dramatic still. Indictable offences known to the police had reached by 1961 a figure of between two and a half and three times what they were in 1938, and nearly 54 per cent. above what they were ten years earlier. True, there have been moments of hope. A slight drop in the total between 1945 and 1946 was followed immediately by a rise and then by a substantial fall which left the 1949 figure lower than any since 1944. After another slight rise in 1950 and a larger one in 1951 a continuous fall was recorded for the next three years, the figure for 1954 being the lowest for ten years; but the effect of this improvement has, alas! been wholly obliterated by the steady and substantial increase which has continued in an unbroken series year by year since 1954.

This increase, moreover, has not been evenly spread over different categories of crime. Known offences of violence against the person have increased to nearly six and a half times the 1938 total, cases of receiving and sex offences to about four times, burglary to between three and four times, and theft and frauds to between two and three times. It almost looks as if the nastiest offences were setting the fastest pace. Among non-indictable offences convictions for drunkenness have risen by nearly 42 per cent. since 1938, the increase having raced ahead in the past 10 years; whilst the increase in traffic offences in the same period, perhaps surprisingly, amounts to only about 50 per cent.; but it is a sobering thought that these last now account for no less than 61.8 per cent. of all the convictions recorded in the criminal courts. In the course of these lectures I shall frequently have occasion to include

---

[1] All the figures in this chapter relate to 1961 or before. Most of them are updated to 1978 in the postscript which follows this chapter (see p. 26).

traffic offences along with other crimes; and for this I make no apology, since not only do these offences occupy a large proportion of the time of the courts, but much of more general application is also to be learned from them.

It is a depressing story. Admittedly the picture presented by the criminal statistics, the whole range and compilation of which are now under review by a Departmental Committee, may be somewhat distorted. But there is very little reason to suppose that the distortion is in the direction of underestimation. And the gloom is not dispelled by the discovery that the harder we try, the less apparently do we succeed. Penal treatments could be described as cumulative failures. The more anyone experiences them, the greater the probability that he will require further treatment still. In their recent study of persistent offenders Hammond and Chayen[2] found that the greater the number of previous court appearances, the greater the risk of reconviction; and this trend was present alike amongst those who had been sentenced to preventive detention and amongst those who, though liable to this sentence, had actually been otherwise dealt with. Out of a group of 318 in the latter class 58 per cent. of those with less than 10 previous court appearances, 71 per cent. of those with 10 to 19 previous appearances and 81 per cent. of those with 20 to 29 previous appearances were reconvicted within a two- to three-year period. Amongst those released from preventive detention[3] the corresponding figures were 55 per cent., 66 per cent., and 63 per cent.—the trend being less marked because the number in the group (108) was not so large.

Of course there is nothing unexpected in this. In the world as it is, the longer one's criminal record, the less the chance of living in any way that does not lengthen it still further. But the trend is worth recording if only because it

[2] Hammond, W. H. and Chayen, E., *Persistent Criminals* (H.M.S.O., 1963), p. 102.

[3] Preventive detention has since been abolished: see Postscript to Chapter 2, p. 55.

is open to more than one interpretation. No doubt it is likewise true that the risk of requiring an operation for cancer is greater in someone who has already undergone one operation for this disease than in one in whom it has not made itself apparent. The nature of the disease is not understood, and the treatment therefore palliative rather than curative: and the same could be true of criminality. At the same time a more sinister interpretation in the case of criminality is also possible—namely, that the treatment itself aggravates the disease.

Meanwhile the sociologically-minded magistrate (and indeed any judicial personage in whom curiosity has not been wholly stilled) will certainly hunger for explanations of the persistence of these ugly blemishes upon an otherwise tolerably civilised society. He will ask himself, first: why do people commit crimes? and secondly, perhaps, why do people refrain from committing them?

To the first of these questions, he will still get but a dusty answer; for aetiological research in criminology tends to be as inconclusive as its volume begins to look impressive. From the crude criminal statistics, the most striking and consistent answers that suggest themselves are that crime is the product of youth and masculinity. At least detected indictable crime is clearly and consistently the special province of the young male. In 1961 87.1 per cent. of all those convicted of indictable offences were males: 10 years earlier the figure was 88.1 per cent.; and in 1938 it stood at 87.7 per cent. If allowance is made for differences in the population at risk, male criminality at all ages (as measured by indictable offences) in 1961 was between seven and eight times as great as that of females, the ratio ranging from 10 to one in the under 14 age group down to rather more than four to one among the over thirties. Ten years earlier the corresponding figures were eight to one at all ages taken together, rather more than 12 to one amongst the under fourteens and nearly five-and-a-half to one for those over 30; whilst in 1938 the ratios stood at more than seven-and-a-half to one at all ages together, at 17 to one in the youngest and at nearly four-and-a-half to one in the oldest age group. Thus it would seem that the overwhelming dominance of the male in this, as in many other fields, although clearly subject to challenge, cannot yet be said to be seriously threatened. Indeed, while for many years now overcrowding in men's prisons has been a persistent nightmare, a not infrequent problem in Holloway Gaol has been the lack of sufficient inmates to keep the place clean.

It is perhaps rather curious that no serious attempt has yet been made to explain the remarkable facts of the sex ratio in detected criminality; for the scale of the sex differential far outranks all the other traits (except that of age in the case of indictable offences) which have been supposed to distinguish the delinquent from the non-deliquent population. I have referred to this before[4] and now do so again because it appears to me that so remarkable a phenomenon has never received the attention that it deserves. It seems to be one of those facts which escapes notice by virtue of its very conspicuousness. It is surely, to say the least, very odd that half the population should be apparently immune to the criminogenic factors which lead to the downfall of so significant a proportion of the other half. Equally odd is it, too, that although the criminological experience of different countries varies considerably, nevertheless the sex differential remains, at least in the more sophisticated areas of the world, everywhere a conspicuous feature. Whether there are exceptions among the underdeveloped communities I would be interested to learn. Yet at least in the world that we know, girls as often as boys may come from broken homes, and stupid, neglectful or indifferent parents have daughters as well as sons; while girls are as likely as boys to be born and brought

[4] Wootton, Barbara, *Social Science and Social Pathology* (Allen and Unwin, 1959), pp. 30, 31.

up in slum sub-cultures. Yet by comparison with their brothers, only rarely are girls found guilty of crimes.

It seems improbable that this difference is of biological origin. If it was, we might as well forget it, as there would be nothing to be done about it short of biological engineering. The scale of the contrast alone renders a biological interpretation unlikely; for the known personality differences between the sexes are not of this order. For example: the range of masculine capacity to perform intelligence tests overlaps that of females at both ends, an excess of males being found both in the highest grades, and among the morons. But overall differences of the order of 17 to one or even of 10 to one are unknown in respect of intelligence or other attributes which are physically and culturally within the reach of both sexes. Clearly some process of cultural conditioning must be at work in the one sex, from which the other is everywhere exempt. To identify this would make possible a larger reduction in criminality than is offered by any other line of inquiry.

This prospect is so alluring that it is worth giving a good deal of thought to methods by which light might be thrown on the question why the sexes behave so differently. Such investigations are not easy to devise. Any differences between the childhood experiences and upbringing of boys and girls are subtle and elusive. But it might, I think, be worth making an intensive study of samples of the minority of women who do commit typically masculine crimes, in order to see if any differences can be detected between them and their more characteristically law-abiding sisters.

Secondly, it would be of interest to know whether female resistance to criminal temptations is due to internal or external sanctions. Do women have a stronger moral sense, and suffer more from the pangs of conscience, or is it just that they are more timid and dare not therefore risk the possible consequences of getting into trouble? It would not, I think, be beyond the bounds of psychological research to look into that question.

In the third place, attention might be focused upon the very large body of women who are now exposed to much the same temptations as men. It used to be said that the more restricted scope of women's lives and activity was at least in part responsible for their modest contribution to offences against property other than shoplifting—yet although the sex ratio appears to be gradually diminishing, it remains a remarkable fact that the mass exodus of women, especially married women, from their homes into outside employment which has been so striking a feature of the past few years should have had so little apparent effect, one way or the other, upon their disposition to criminal behaviour. Why do they not copy, or share, their husbands' and colleagues' stealing?

Perhaps also a useful fourth line of inquiry might be to examine more closely some of the outstanding differences as between one class of offence and another. Out of the 200 categories into which the Home Office divides the various items in the criminal calendar, adult female convictions actually outnumber those of males only in the following: infanticide, procuring abortion, concealment of birth, offences of prostitution, cruelty to children, brothel keeping and theft from shops and stalls. Of these, infanticide and offences connected with prostitution are not crimes with which a man can be charged, and the reasons for female predominance in all the others are perhaps not far to seek. In all cases except offences of prostitution and shoplifting, the numbers involved are quite small; but it is perhaps of interest that in the last-named, which is far and away the commonest female crime, the feminine lead is not established until after the age of 17. Small boys are much more addicted to shoplifting than are their sisters, even if their Mums are twice as likely to get into trouble for this offence as are their Dads.[5]

In the remaining categories in which male convictions predominate, the size of the differential varies very greatly.

[5] But see Postscript to this chapter, p. 29.

Women are less liable to conviction for murder, manslaughter or causing death by reckless driving, whilst at the other end of the scale adult male convictions for drunkenness, simple and aggravated (a luxury which women perhaps cannot afford?), are nearly fourteen times as frequent as those of females. Indeed all the variations, as between one type of offence and another, are both numerous and fascinating, and it may well be that a detailed analysis, tracing any changes in the differential through time, and relating these to the changes in the roles of the sexes in our culture, might provide some useful clues.

Meanwhile age patterns show a similar broad consistency, although the incidence of particular offences at certain ages seems to be changing. While the great majority of the total of offences is committed by adults, the share of the young seems lately to have increased, the proportion of convictions of all kinds above the age of twenty-one having dropped from 82 per cent. in 1951 to 75 per cent. 10 years later; and in the case of indictable offences the accent on youth is very much more pronounced. The age at which the findings of guilt for these offences reaches its peak in proportion to the population at risk is now 14 for both sexes. Ten years ago it was 14 for males and 13 for females, while in 1938 it was 13 for males but 19 for females. As we have seen, however, the female contribution to the total is so small that their relative instability makes very little difference to the final result. Taking both sexes together in 1961, 52.2 per cent. of all those convicted of indictable crimes were under 21 years old; in 1951 the proportion was 46.4 per cent.: in 1938 it stood at about 50.5 per cent.; and the proportion of indictable offenders of an age to be dealt with in the juvenile courts, which today amounts to a little over one-third of the total convictions, is still almost exactly the same as it was ten years ago, and the same too as in the year before the war.[6]

If the sex differential is unexplained, attempts to build

[6] See Postscript to this chapter, p. 29, for later figures.

theories of criminality in terms of immaturity have an awkward way of resolving themselves into tautologies. From the facts already given it is clear that a substantial proportion of indictable crimes is committed by the young and that a high proportion of youthful offenders mend their ways as they advance in years; and Dr. Terence Willett[7] has shown that the same is true of certain types of motoring offence, notably driving whilst disqualified or without insurance. Older persons who commit similar offences are, therefore, behaving in a fashion that is more characteristic of the young: but to say that their criminality is due to immaturity is merely to restate this fact in different terms.

It might, however, be worth while to examine in detail differences between the offences committed by the young and those for which their elders are responsible—and more particularly between young offenders and those whose first conviction is acquired later in life; for it seems likely, and there is, I think, some evidence to support the view, that the psycho-social aspects may be quite different in the two cases. The young thief or house-breaker, for instance, is more often merely conforming to the *mores* of his social group (it used to be: "we might as well do a bit of house-breaking before we go in the army") while in the case of the older offender (other than the professional recidivist), a crime seems more often to be the result of some incidental personal disaster—such as a marital breakdown or a spell of unemployment.

Why then do we know so little? Mainly, I think, through failure to appreciate the heterogeneity of the phenomena recorded in the bald tables of the criminal statistics, and through the persistent influence of the stereotype of "the criminal" or "the delinquent," with its implication that all persons found guilty of breaches of the criminal law must, if we only look long enough and hard enough, reveal characteristics that distinguish them from the rest of the

[7] Willett, T. C., *Criminal on the Road* (Tavistock Publications, 1964).

population. Yet the heterogeneity of criminal behaviour should surely be obvious enough. Even if attention is confined to what are generally thought of as "traditional" or "real" crimes, the variety of actions covered even by a single category in the official calendar is immense. The underpaid clerk who takes a subsidy from the firm's cash-box, meaning to put it back when he gets his wages at the end of the week, is far removed alike from the professional pickpocket, from the child who steals from a sweet-shop for the devil of it, and from the compulsive stealer of women's underwear: yet all are guilty of theft. Equally great is the distance between the mercy-killer who gives an overdose to an incurable invalid, the exasperated husband who strangles a nagging wife after years of marital misery and the brutal murderer who bludgeons a man to death in order to rifle his savings. And of course if horizons are widened to include every kind of offence which may be the subject of a criminal charge, the heterogeneity becomes far more obvious. Anyone might fairly be sceptical about the search for the distinctive common characteristics of the professional safe-breaker and the motorist who parks his car in a prohibited place—other than the obvious one that each in his own measure prefers his personal advantage to the convenience of others.

Nor is heterogeneity merely a matter of the variety of types of offence. I have already called attention to possible differences between the young and the old, and it is vital to remember also that the criminal statistics may be swollen either by the increasingly persistent criminality of persons with already one or more convictions, or, alter-natively, by the spread of law-breaking to wider circles of the population. Unfortunately, present sources of information do not enable us to say in what proportions each of these two trends has contributed to the con-temporary scene. But at least it should be clear that each constitutes a totally different social problem and that the causes of recidivism and the causes of first offences cannot all be lumped together under the single heading: causes of crimes.

Admittedly, persons who are convicted of one type of offence show a significant tendency to incur convictions also for offences of other types, and this fact might be read as evidence of an inherent, generalised disposition towards criminality. Such a tendency has been demonstrated for sexual offences by the Cambridge Institute of Criminology, and for a certain group of motoring offences by Dr. Willett. In the case of sexual offenders, the Cambridge investigation[8] showed that out of a total of nearly 2,000 sex offenders covered by the investigation, one in four had at least one other conviction for a non-sexual offence (mostly breaking or theft) by the end of a follow-up period of four years from their first conviction. Again Dr. Willett[9] found that in a sample of 653 "serious" motoring offenders in the Home Counties, more than one-fifth had a "criminal record" also for non-motoring offences, the proportion varying from 5.1 per cent. of those who had failed to stop after an accident to 24 per cent. of those convicted of insurance offences and 77 per cent. of those found guilty of driving whilst disqualified.

The weight of these facts, however, as evidence of any inherent disposition towards criminal behaviour as such, is much reduced, so far as the sexual offenders are concerned, by the facts that persons known to the police are always likely suspects for any subsequent crime; that one conviction, and still more one period of imprisonment, is a great impediment to a subsequent honest and respectable living; and that the experience of conviction, and still more of imprisonment, is itself only too likely to be criminogenic. Dr. Willett's material, moreover, is heavily coloured by the predominance in his list of "serious" motoring offences, of the two crimes of driving whilst disqualified or

---

[8] Cambridge Department of Criminal Science, *Sexual Offences* (Macmillan) 1957, p. 315.

[9] Willett, *op. cit.*

without proper insurance, which are by their nature more akin to "ordinary" crimes than to other driving offences.

We must, I think, conclude that in view of the heterogeneity of contemporary crimes, the concept of the "criminal" or the "delinquent" is seldom meaningful; and that it is to be regretted that these stereotypes continue to haunt discussion at both the expert and the popular level. Rather might it have been expected that the invention of the internal combustion engine, with the consequent revelation of the extremely widespread disposition to violate one or other item in the criminal code, might have put paid to them once and for all. Now that traffic offences constitute over 60 per cent. of all convictions, the discriminating power of the fact of conviction, irrespective of the nature or circumstances of the offence, must be reckoned as negligible. Indeed if the term "criminal" is to be used at all as a descriptive noun, its application should be confined to the professional, or at least to the habitual, offender who makes crime (presumably in the form of property offences) his normal mode of getting a living.

The abandonment of the terms "criminal" and "delinquent" would, moreover, have the virtue of discouraging what has long been a standard but thoroughly unfruitful pattern of criminological research, in which a group of undifferentiated "delinquents" is compared in respect of certain personal or social characteristics with a matched control group of "non-delinquents." The hypothesis that such a group will reveal more inherent distinctive characteristics than, say, a sample of hereditary peers or of the winners of premium bonds grows more and more improbable; and the search for these characteristics is constantly vitiated by more than one highly dubious assumption. It is vitiated, first, by the assumption that the "delinquent" subjects studied are reasonably representative of the whole population of offenders of like age and sex. Yet not only is selection unavoidably biased by the fact that one can only study the detected offender: an even graver distortion is introduced if, as often happens, the subjects are selected from the inmates of penal institutions such as prisons or remand homes. No one with any experience of sentencing procedure can fail to be conscious of the enormous element of luck that enters into the decision as to who is and who is not to be deprived of his liberty. Indeed I need only remind you that, as Roger Hood[10] has revealed, the proportion of adult men imprisoned for indictable offences in any one of the four years 1951-54 by different English courts varied between three per cent. and 55 per cent.; and that in a sample of 12 urban courts sentencing adult men for comparable offences of dishonesty in the same period the imprisonment rate as between one group of courts and another ranged from about 50 per cent. to under 15 per cent.

Secondly, the assumption that members of control groups of "non-delinquents" are in fact innocent of criminal offences is apt to be much too lightly made. In his study of the members of a Liverpool city youth club Dr. Mays[11] found reason to believe that at least three-quarters of his whole sample had in fact committed offences, although less than half had actually been found guilty by the courts. Yet Dr. Andry[12] in his investigation into delinquency and parental pathology apparently took no pains to ensure that his "non-delinquent" control group had not in fact ever been guilty of stealing, on the ground that some stealing of "a relatively harmless and non-persistent order is indulged in by many boys": nor does he appear to regard his results as in any way invalidated by the fact that no less than 68 per cent.[13] of his controls admitted to having stolen at some time.

In the third place—and this is perhaps most questionable

[10] Hood, Roger, *Sentencing in Magistrates' Courts* (Stevens, 1962), p. 12.

[11] Mays, J. B., *Growing Up in the City* (University of Liverpool Press, 1954), pp. 77, 81.

[12] Andry, R. G., *Delinquency and Parental Pathology* (Methuen, 1960), p. 11.

[13] *Ibid.* p. 94.

of all—it is too often assumed that any detectable difference between the convicted and the unconvicted must be due to the inherent qualities of the former and not to their unique experience. Yet all convicted persons, and more particularly all those who have been imprisoned, have suffered one highly significant experience which the innocent and the undetected guilty alike escape; and it is at least a possibility that it is to that experience that any peculiarities which they exhibit may in part be due. That this possibility is nearly always ignored is as understandable as it is methodologically lamentable. To admit it would be too grave an admission of the failure of our penal system. But I may remind you that Dr. Field in an unpublished investigation into the personality of recidivists concluded that certain of the psychological tests which distinguish criminals from the rest of the population appear to be "more heavily weighted by the consequence of asocial actions than by incapacitating personality attributes"[14]; and that both the extreme rigidity found to be characteristic of many persistent offenders and crime itself might be comparable to iatrogenic disease.

Altogether it is hardly surprising that this omnibus type of criminological research has yielded such trivial results. The further it is carried and the greater the refinement of the methods of investigation used, the more closely does any group of miscellaneous criminals appear to resemble the population at large.[15] For the causes of crime might not unreasonably be compared in their variety to the causes of, say, letter-writing. Except that they are literate and articulate, letter-writers are unlikely to share many peculiar characteristics; and the occasions on which, and the subjects about which, they take up their pens are probably not much more miscellaneous than are the occasions on

[14] Field, J. G., *Report to the Prison Commission of an Investigation into the Personality of Recidivists* (1960), unpublished.

[15] For a summary of some of the evidence on this see Wootton, Barbara, *Social Science and Social Pathology* (Allen and Unwin, 1959), pp. 301 *et seq.*

which, and the endlessly varied circumstances in which, a crime is committed.[16]

In this connection we might, I think, have something to learn from medical parallels. In medicine certain environmental conditions are recognised as generally conducive to good health: or perhaps it would be safer to say that the absence of certain conditions is likely to foster disease. Infant mortality is higher in the slums than in the green and airy spaces of suburbia; while poor nutrition results in a variety of what are known as deficiency diseases. Equally is it apparent that individuals vary in their innate resistance to illness: there is such a thing as a sound constitution. But such broad generalisations conceal very much more complex relationships between environmental conditions and specific diseases: it is possible to make oneself ill by over- as well as under-eating, and the vital statistics show that the incidence of certain diseases is heavier amongst the well-to-do than amongst the poor. In medicine, therefore, one hears less about the causes of disease than about the causes of diseases; and criminologists would also, I suggest, equally benefit by the use of the plural rather than of the singular, and by thinking always in specific, rather than in general, terms.

It may be that there are other lessons also to be learned from medicine. In criminology a feud sometimes of almost theological intensity divides those who favour sociological from those disposed to psychological explanations; and, despite many pious aspirations, interdisciplinary enterprises are all too seldom successfully launched. Everyone recognises that both sociology and psychology have something to contribute to the understanding of various forms of criminal behaviour; yet the contribution of each is too often measured, alike by its advocates and its adversaries, less in terms of its pragmatic usefulness than by its claim to be an expression of absolute truth. In

[16] For later examples of more rigorously controlled researches see Postscript to this chapter, pp. 20 and 29.

medicine a more practical attitude seems to prevail. Although the cause of every case of illness, no less than of every crime, is to be found in the interaction of a person (who is himself the product of the interaction of heredity and environment) with an environmental situation, and although in both cases causation is always multiple, in medicine practical considerations appear more commonly to govern the decision upon which causal element emphasis is laid. The factor designated as the "cause" of a disease is the one which is thought most likely to be amenable to treatment. So in the event of an outbreak of typhoid, attention is directed not to personal susceptibility to the infection (which doubtless varies as in other diseases from one individual to another) but rather to suspected drains or an ice-cream factory, whilst in a smallpox epidemic priority is given to investigation of the possible contacts of the victim with other infected persons, and in cases of gastric ulcer to the patient's susceptibility to nervous stress or perhaps to his diet. Undoubtedly in every instance both a personal and an environmental factor must be present: no epidemic attacks everybody who is at risk. But it is the likely chances of prevention or cure which alone determine where, in each instance, emphasis is laid.

It is to be hoped, therefore, that narrower and more specific investigations will hereafter take the place of the omnibus researches into crime or delinquency which have hitherto been so popular—and so unproductive. And already a welcome trend in this direction is apparent. To mention only a few recent examples, we have Gibbens and Prince's investigation into Shoplifters[17]; the Home Office Research Unit's Reports on Persistent Offenders,[18] and on Murder[19]; and the Cambridge Institute of Criminology's

---

[17] Gibbens, T. C. N. and Prince, J. *Shoplifting* (Institute for the Study and Treatment of Delinquency, 1962).

[18] Hammond, W. H. and Chayen, E., *Persistent Criminals* (H.M.S.O., 1963).

[19] Gibson, E. and Klein, S., *Murder* (H.M.S.O., 1961).

studies of Robbery,[20] of Sexual Offenders,[21] and of the Habitual Prisoner.[22] Each of these gives an insight into the endless variety of a particular category of crime or of a particular group of offenders. Each of these inquiries illustrates, too, the multiplicity of circumstances which give rise to outwardly similar forms of behaviour; and each marks a step away from the almost childishly simple, generalised theories of the past towards the vastly more complex and more specialised hypotheses which alone can be expected to achieve even a rough approximation to reality. For, if the causes of crime are as manifold as the causes of letter-writing, the causes of particular crimes are probably not less miscellaneous than those of, let us say, the letters that are written to the Press.

Every crime, let us not forget, is committed by a person who might not have committed it. He might not have committed it had he been born with a different genetic constitution: he might not have committed it if his parents had treated him differently, or if he had been brought up in a different neighbourhood; he might not have committed it if he had not happened at the time to be particularly short of money or if he had not had the misfortune to run into "bad company"; and he might not have committed it if he had been differently treated on the occasion of a previous offence, or if his chances of employment had not been ruined by his previous record. Even "the precipitating or trigger-pulling factors" may themselves have a specificity of their own—as Dr. Peter Scott, whose wisdom in these matters may be said to be matched only by the breadth of his experience, has reminded us in a recent article, quoting in illustration the cases of the "inadequate-feeling adolescent who only commits offences in response to a direct challenge to his manliness; the young man who only

[20] McClintock, F. H. and Gibson, E., *Robbery in London* (Macmillan, 1961).
[21] Cambridge Institute of Criminology, *Sexual Offences* (Macmillan, 1957).
[22] West, D. J., *The Habitual Prisoner* (Macmillan, 1963).

commits an assault when his advances are rejected; the indecent exposer who never offends except against a background of increasing marital tension."[2 3] Hitherto, however, owing no doubt to the influence of the stereotype of the "criminal"—to the belief that any offender must somehow be "different"—the immediate precipitating circumstances have not, I think, had their proper share of attention. Yet to neglect them is like trying to tackle a smallpox epidemic without bothering about people's contacts.

Instructive, also, in this context, is the contrast between the concealed premises of investigations into accidents on the one hand and those concerned with the causes of crime on the other hand. In an aeroplane or train accident, the cause is normally sought in the immediate circumstances, rather than in any underlying physical or psychological abnormality in the persons concerned; and these circumstances are accordingly examined with the utmost thoroughness. If indeed a particular person proves to be involved in repeated incidents, attention may be shifted to a study of the reasons for his accident-proneness; but this is exceptional. Normal practice is rather to search, in the first instance, for some particular feature of, or occurrence in, the immediate situation, such as a mechanical failure, a casual error of judgment or a climatic disturbance: whereas students of crime, if they do not neglect the immediate circumstances altogether, generally look first for personal peculiarities in the individuals concerned.

However, as research becomes increasingly specific, one may hope that it will uncover more and more recognisable and recurring patterns, in which particular types of person are found to commit particular types of crime in particular types of circumstance. But such are the subtleties and complexities of human behaviour, and so numerous are the variables of which account must in every instance be taken,

---

[2 3] Scott, P. D., "Delinquency: Types and Causes," *The Howard Journal* (1962), Vol. XI, No. 1.

that the evolution of satisfactory theories may well have to wait upon the success with which the electronic computer can be called to the aid of the human mind.

Meanwhile, the questing magistrate may turn to the alternative question—Why do we refrain from committing crimes? How, in fact, is the standing miracle of the socialisation of the savage human infant so often successfully accomplished?

Here both positive and negative factors clearly have their place, though it is the negative which have enjoyed the greater share of attention. Among the latter, the origins of those powerful inhibitions, conscience and the sense of guilt, have been extensively studied by psychologists, and Freudian, or quasi-Freudian, theories appear to hold the field. The capacity to experience guilt, it seems, has to be acquired in infancy, if at all, since it is thought to derive from the child's discovery that parents withdraw their cherished affection on the occasions of his wrongdoing. If you do not catch it young, you have but a poor chance of catching it at all. It is moreover a capacity which is known to vary from one individual to another in accordance with temperament, perhaps also with physique (the fat being apparently less susceptible than the thin) and[24] with infantile experience; and those who have no loving parents may miss it altogether. These last, however, though familiar enough to every magistrate who has been faced (and which of us has not?) with the wholly egocentric institutionalised adolescent, or with the child who steals objects to compensate for lack of the affection that he has never had—these cases are clearly quite exceptional. Somehow or other most of us, happily, whether fat or thin, do manage to acquire some degree of susceptibility to guilt.

But the crucial question then arises as to the particular actions to which the sense of guilt becomes attached; and to this hitherto less attention has been paid. To this

[24] See Argyle, M., "Delinquency and Morals," *The Listener*, June 21, 1962.

question the answer, in any individual case, would seem to be dependent on both sociological and psychological factors; for the process by which the performance of particular actions comes to be frowned upon by the *mores* of any group or society is clearly social; whilst the acceptance or rejection by any individual of the accepted moral code must itself be a matter of his personal psychology.

About neither aspect are we, as yet, well informed. But what we do know is that codes vary greatly from class to class. In some circles, for example, housebreaking, in Dr. Gibbens'[25] apt phrase, has become "culturally conventional"; though even in these storebreaking tends to be regarded as an even more innocent pastime. Again, theft from public bodies may fail to evoke a single qualm in those who would hesitate to steal from a known person; while stealing from one's employer, which is generally regarded by the law as exceptionally heinous, is to many of those who engage in it simply a method of rectifying the blatant injustices of the wage structure. Recent experience has taught us, too (as the Americans also learned in the prohibition epoch), that in all social classes a sense of guilt has almost completely failed to attach itself to some of the—literally—most deadly and destructive of all contemporary offences. With the possible exception of drunken driving, hardly any guilt[26] today attaches to motoring offences, even those of a quite deliberate nature which cannot be laughed off as due to incompetence or carelessness. Of the 653 serious motoring offenders covered by Dr. Willett's[27] investigation three-quarters are said to have taken the view that there is nothing wrong in breaking the motoring law if

[25] Gibbens, T. C. N., *Psychiatric Studies of Borstal Lads* (O.U.P., 1963), p. 21.

[26] I use the term here, of course, in its psychological, not its legal, sense. The feeling of guilt evoked by an outraged conscience has, of course, nothing to do with the presence or absence of *mens rea*, about which I shall have much to say in my next lecture.

[27] *The Observer*, May 12, 1963.

you can get away with it; and even the police themselves appear to be disposed to regard motoring offenders as "normal respectable chaps." In Scotland a few years ago a man who was actually serving a sentence of imprisonment for drunken driving was appointed while still in prison to an administrative post in a public corporation[28]—in striking contrast to the late Dr. Joad whose public career was ruined by conviction for an offence of dishonesty for which a sentence of imprisonment was not, and indeed could not legally have been, imposed. Even the courts themselves seem to be not indisposed towards similar attitudes. Drunken and dangerous driving by a veterinary surgeon—who was, moreover, an admitted alcoholic—has been held apparently not to amount to professionally disgraceful conduct[29]; and I have heard a judge in the Crown Court observe on hearing an offender's record: "It's a traffic offence: I don't think we need worry about that"; while the practice of producing details only of offences other than motoring is by no means unusual. Significant also is the case of Donald Smith. In 1961 this man,[30] who had previously been convicted of breaking offences, was found guilty of a breach of probation on account of convictions for careless driving, failing to report an accident, driving uninsured and driving without L-plates and without supervision. For each of these offences a moderate fine had been imposed by the magistrates; but for the breach the Recorder of Portsmouth sentenced Smith to 12 months' imprisonment. Yet on appeal this sentence was revoked as being "wrong in principle," and a further period of probation substituted, on the ground that the driving offences were not in any sense offences of dishonesty, and that, although not trivial, they were of a "minor character." The sentence may indeed well have been thought to be excessively severe, but what, one

[28] *The Times*, January 11, 1958.
[29] *Re Hans, The Times*, October 12, 1960.
[30] *R.* v. *Smith, The Times*, March 7, 1961.

would like to know, was the principle which it violated?

The attachment of a sense of guilt to particular actions, no less than the genesis of the sense of guilt itself, must, in the view of some psychologists, be formed in infancy if it is to be effective. In a broadcast talk last year,[31] Michael Argyle emphasised that people tend to feel guilty about what was prohibited in childhood—as, for example, being greedy or using rude words, rather than about such adult misdemeanours as drunken driving; and from this he inferred that little reliance can be placed on the sense of guilt, since "Guilt feelings are experienced by the wrong people for the wrong things." Such a conclusion seems, however, to be unduly pessimistic and to arise only from an unduly restricted choice of examples. Granted that it is difficult to make a child too young to drive feel guilty about drunken motoring, most law-abiding parents surely manage to stop their children from stealing. If few adults seem to be inhibited in the use of rude words, many more (at least in certain circles) would be deeply ashamed of stealing or of using personal violence; and these attitudes, too, can equally well be traced back to childhood. Nevertheless the hypothesis that particular codes, as distinct from the moral sense itself, are only acceptable if acquired in childhood must, pending further researches, still be regarded as unproven.

An alternative and currently popular explanation holds that it is the function of religion to forge the link between conscience and society's moral code; and that it is to the decay of religious belief that we must look to explain the apparent absence of guilt or remorse amongst many young offenders who are otherwise no more psychopathic than the speeding motorist in the built-up area. Certainly no one can read much Victoriana without being deeply impressed by the difference from our own of the mental climate of an age in which such Christian dogmas as the

[31] Argyle, M., "Delinquency and Morals," *The Listener*, June 21, 1962.

Virgin birth, the divinity of Christ, the resurrection and the certain promise of personal immortality commanded general and literal acceptance; and in which these doctrines provided a supernatural sanction for moral codes.

That a vacuum, even a dangerous vacuum, has been thus created cannot, I think, be denied. Where opinions may differ is as to how this should be filled. The churches, naturally, seek to forge afresh the link between morality and religion; but they can only fight a rearguard action: disbelief has gone too far. Indeed eminent dignitaries in the Church itself no longer even pretend to believe all the traditional Christian doctrines. Yet to the public at large those doctrines are still offered at their face value; and still the moral training of the young, in school, in church and in religious broadcasting, relies upon them for its sanctions.

To generations reared in a scientific age those sanctions no longer have validity, unless for a tiny minority of convinced believers: to the rest the Christian story is a fairy story. Our prisons are not peopled with renegade Christians: they are peopled with practising agnostics for whom the moral vacuum can only be filled by a humanistic morality, demanding no extra-scientific or supernatural assumptions; and this their inmates are not offered. Yet a secular society which does not have the courage to evolve, and to propagate, a secular morality must not be surprised if it finds itself devoid of any morality at all.

Conscience and the sense of guilt are, however, at best but negative incentives—they inhibit vice rather than attract to virtue. In more positive terms, may not crimes result, less from the failure of inhibitions, than from the absence of sufficiently alluring alternatives? In the words of Professor Sprott: "If only we could discover how to make law-abidingness attractive to offenders we would not send naughty boys to detention centres, where the Spartan regime is hardly calculated to demonstrate the dazzling charms of being good."[32]

[32] Sprott, W. J. H., "Society and Criminology," *The Howard Journal* (1961), Vol. X., No. 4.

Surprisingly, perhaps, the aetiology of crime is seldom discussed in these positive terms. Yet in a world in which ambition and self-advancement rank as virtues, in which money, prestige and influence all go together, the legal roads to approved social goals are still far from equally open to all. To travel the path from, say, medical student to consultant calls for skill, ability and industry, and progress along it is unlikely to be expedited by illegal means; and for those who follow this road to the end income will rise step by step up to a mature age. For those too who are already possessed of capital, or for the lucky few on whom nature has bestowed the peculiar qualities that constitute a flair for business, wealth can be dramatically multiplied. But for the majority whose endowment, natural or material, is undistinguished, opportunity is still restricted, and on many the mark of failure has been imprinted even before they are ten years old by a highly competitive educational system. Available jobs are uninteresting and the maximum wage is likely to be reached by the age of twenty-one. For such as these, not surprisingly, the attraction of crime is the "enthusiasm and excitement"[33] so sadly lacking elsewhere.

The "affluent" society is not affluent. It derives that name rather from its esteem of affluence; and the prizes which it offers, though unequally distributed, are nevertheless not wholly unattainable. In that, it differs, alike from the aristocratic society from which it has emerged, and from the "meritocracy," or, as I would rather say, the "cephalocracy" (since there can be no merit in being born with brains), into which it would seem to be merging. Crime cannot alter the rank into which you were born, nor can it get you brains. But it can and does get you money.

---

[33] "The main feature distinguishing all successful offenders, whether first offenders operating on their own, or associating with more experienced contemporaries or older professional criminals, is enthusiasm and excitement"; Gibbens, T. C. N., *Psychiatric Studies of Borstal Lads* (O.U.P., 1963), p. 20.

A highly competitive, socially hierarchical, acquisitive society offers in fact an ideal breeding-ground for crimes against property; just as a mechanistic, speed-besotted age is a standing invitation to motorised violence.

The judge or magistrate who reflects on all this will no doubt share the regret but not, perhaps, so much the pained surprise of the authors of the White Paper on Penal Policy,[34] when they wrote of the "disquieting feature of our society that . . . rising standards in material prosperity, education and social welfare have brought no decrease in the high rate of crime reached during the war"; nor will he be surprised that the crimes of affluent America, like so many others of her products, are bigger and better than those of other peoples. Indeed he may conclude, with Sir Thomas More, that "if you do not remedy the conditions which produced thieves, the vigorous execution of justice in punishing them will be in vain," and, with Henry Fielding, he may marvel that offenders are not even more numerous than they are. And perhaps, too, he will be moved to question how far in such a society the criminal procedure of which he is himself a part is adapted to discharge the heavy tasks now imposed upon it.

To that question I shall address myself in the lecture that follows.

[34]*Penal Practice in a Changing Society*, Cmnd. 645 (H.M.S.O.) 1959.

Since my lectures were delivered, the material in the Home Office annual volume on *Criminal Statistics* (England and Wales) has been greatly elaborated and expanded, although the changes have not been obviously much influenced by the 1967 Report of the Departmental Committee on Criminal Statistics referred to on p. 31. In consequence it is not possible to update the figures relating to the volume and nature of criminal acts in exactly the form in which these appeared in my original lecture. But it is at least clear that, in spite of the many legislative changes and researches (not to mention 17 further courses of Hamlyn lectures) which have occupied the intervening period, the trend towards an ever-increasing volume of crime has continued unabated, nor have there been many significant changes in the pattern of criminality.

Thus, the number of persons convicted of offences of all kinds has risen from 1,152,397 in 1961 to 1,933,567 in 1978, while the number found guilty of *indictable* crimes has increased from 182,217 to 424,029. These figures of course represent only a fraction of the offences recorded by the police, in many of which either no one is prosecuted or the prosecution does not succeed. Indictable crimes recorded by the police have risen spectacularly from 870,894 in 1961 to 2,395,757 in 1978, that is, from 1,878 to 4,878 per 1,000,000 of population. But there have still been rare moments of hope. Between 1972 and 1973 the total dropped by about 32,000, but rose again in the two following years passing the two million mark in 1975, to reach a peak of 2,463,025 in 1977, but dropping back again in 1978 to the total of 2,395,757 just quoted.

Within these omnibus figures there has been a five-fold increase in recorded crimes of violence since 1961.

Burglaries and robberies appear to have increased about three-and-a-half times, theft and handling stolen goods about two-and-a-half times, while fraud and forgery have trebled; but in the three last-named groups redefinition and reclassification make comparisons not entirely reliable. On the other hand recorded sexual offences have increased by barely ten per cent. since 1961; but this figure again probably does not tell the whole truth, particularly in relation to the more serious offences. For example, in 1961 the police recorded 503 cases of rape as against 1,243 in 1978.

Among non-indictable offences, the story is much the same, but for these we have to use conviction figures, as police records (even where they exist) are not published in the Home Office annual *Criminal Statistics*. Since 1961 the number of persons convicted of motoring offences has nearly trebled (partly of course owing to new legislation such as the blood alcohol test) and now accounts for about 90 per cent. of all convictions for breaches of the criminal law, indictable or non-indictable.

This prompts me to call attention to the practice, which I see and greatly deplore, of regarding motoring offences as not "real crimes." Some of those in the non-indictable category are of course trivial, as are other types of offence in that class, *e.g.* failure to hold a valid dog licence or sleeping out. But some motoring offences even in the non-indictable category are potentially, if not actually, serious. Thus, the motorist who passes a red light at night and encounters no other vehicle may get away with a modest fine for failure to comply with traffic directions, when only luck has saved him from the indictable offence of causing death by reckless driving.

In 1965 the Law Society sponsored a Memorandum proposing that a distinction should be drawn between mere "breaches of the Road Traffic Acts" on the one hand and "deliberate conscious, or vicious breaches of the law and reckless acts or omission" on the other; and that the former should be taken out of the criminal jurisdiction altogether, classified as "traffic breaches," and dealt with in special traffic courts where conviction would "not be categorised as criminal."

Into which category then would my red light violator fall, in the event that he encountered no other vehicle or person? (Incidentally no similar suggestion has to my knowledge been made about removing the criminal stigma from other minor offences. When it was proposed that all small thefts should be triable only by magistrates' courts, Parliament would not stand for it. A former Lord Chancellor, the late Lord Dilhorne, remarked at the time that "a petty offence of theft . . . may prevent a young man from taking up a particular profession or occupation . . . because society regards dishonesty as a serious offence, irrespective of the amount of money that has been taken)."[1] On this principle it would follow that a conviction for driving with an excess blood-alcohol level is not a serious offence.

Most remarkable of all, however, in this context is the practice of the Home Office in regard to the offence of causing death by reckless driving. This offence is duly listed in the annual volume of *Criminal Statistics* amongst other indictable offences of violence against the person. Yet in the special chapter on homicides it is not covered, although convictions for causing death by dangerous driving regularly exceeded the annual total for murder and for all forms of manslaughter and infanticide put together, until the substitution of the word "reckless" for "dangerous" reduced the convictions from 450 in 1977 to 293 in 1978. In face of all this, one cannot help suspecting that the tendency to "play down" motoring offences is not unconnected with the fact that they are more commonly committed by persons of superior social status than are other types of crime.

My lecture's statement that the crude criminal statistics suggest that crime is mainly the product of masculine

[1] House of Lords Official Report, January 27, 1977, col. 686.

youth still remains substantially true, although the trend towards sex equality is making its mark in the context of criminality as well as elsewhere. Among persons found guilty of indictable crimes the masculine proportion has fallen from 87 per cent. in 1961 to about 84 per cent. in 1978, but the differential still declines as age advances. It is also still true that people under 21 account for well over half of all convictions for indictable offences. On the other hand, the 17 year-olds have now a higher proportion of such convictions than any other age group, whereas in 1961 that unenviable record was held by youngsters of 14. (Changes in juvenile court procedure have, however, probably affected the figures for those under 17).

One of the most remarkable developments of recent years has been the sex change in shoplifting. Although small boys continue to be more often found guilty of stealing from shops and stalls than are their sisters, it is no longer true that "their Mums are twice as likely to get into trouble for this offence as their Dads." In the magistrates' courts in 1978 male convictions for shoplifting out-numbered those of females at all ages up to 21. Above that age women gained a lead of a mere 270 in a total of over 24,000 cases for each sex, but this is not enough to balance the masculine majority in the younger age groups. Moreover in the Crown Court, where the number of shop-lifters sentenced is much smaller, men are always in a sub-stantial majority. So, somewhat surprisingly, it appears that when all the facts are put together, shoplifting is no longer a feminine speciality in which males are only minority participants. Clearly the men are learning.

On the need for more researches into particular forms of crime rather than into "delinquency" or "delinquents" in general, progress continues to be made; and more care is nowadays taken to see that in comparisons between delin-quents and controls the latter do not include persons guilty of undisclosed offences. An outstanding example of recent work in these respects is William Belson's monu-mental work on *Juvenile Theft: The Causal Factors*

(Harper and Row, 1975). Amongst other important findings, this established that at least occasional stealing by schoolboys is almost universal, the difference between social classes being not whether, but what or how, they steal.

Finally I should like to emphasise one development which I think has played a part in the increase of what are often called "motiveless" or "senseless" crimes, such as vandalism, and many unprovoked attacks on individuals or groups. Although large sections of the population have always been employed in boring or disagreeable jobs, offering little prospect of advancement, this way of life becomes increasingly unacceptable in a world which purports to uphold the doctrine that Jack is as good as his master, and then in practice does precious little to give effect to that presumption. "Mindless crime" may well be the unconscious protest of working-class youths who no longer "know" (or are indeed expected to know) "their place" in Victorian terms, but nevertheless find scant opportunity within the law to achieve the affluence that is widely recognised as both the reward of merit and the hallmark of social prestige.

Chapter 2

THE FUNCTION OF THE COURTS:
PENAL OR PREVENTIVE?

Before I embark on discussion of the function of the criminal courts perhaps a word may be said about the atmosphere in which this function is performed. It is, in the higher courts at least, an atmosphere of archaic majesty and ritual. Moreover the members of the Bar, whether on or off the Bench, constitute a sodality that is, surely, unique among English professions; nor is there anything in their training which might widen their social horizons or enlarge their social observations. In consequence, there is perhaps no place in English life where the divisions of our society are more obtrusive: nowhere where one is more conscious of the division into "them" and "us." Of the effect of this each must judge for himself. Many of those who gave evidence before the Streatfeild Committee[1] expressed the view (though the Committee itself maintained a sceptical attitude) that the formality of the superior courts, along with the period of waiting before trial and the risk of incurring a substantial sentence, had a salutary effect upon offenders. There may indeed be cases where this is so. But my own opinion is that an opposite effect is more often likely: that the formal and unfamiliar language, the wigs and robes, the remoteness of the judge from the lives and temptations of many defendants detract from, rather than add to, the effectiveness of British justice.

But, be that as it may, of the twin functions of the courts in identifying and dealing with (here I deliberately choose what I hope is a wholly neutral word) offenders,

[1] Interdepartmental Committee on the Business of the Criminal Courts, *Report* (H.M.S.O.) 1961, Cmnd. 1289, para. 93.

the first raises fewer controversies than the second. Yet even here certain of the customary procedures seem incongruous in a scientific age.

For instance, the legal process of examination, cross-examination and re-examination can hardly be rated highly as an instrument for ascertaining the facts of past history. At least no scientist would expect to extract the truth from opposite distortions, although it is perhaps not unknown for scientific controversies to resolve themselves —I nearly said degenerate—to this level. The accusatorial method is, however, so deeply rooted in our history that it would be idle to embark on any comparison of its merits with those of its inquisitorial rival. I will therefore only call attention in passing to a former Lord Chancellor's observation (though in a totally different context) that "where the task of a body is to ascertain what has happened, there is not, as far as I can see, any escape from an inquisitorial procedure"[2]—with its implication that in the courts the ascertainment of the facts cannot be the primary concern. That the place of historical truth in the legal process is indeed only secondary is no doubt acceptable legal doctrine—otherwise it would scarcely be possible for a distinguished lawyer to express his admiration of the success of another distinguished lawyer in obtaining an "almost impossible" verdict, as Lord Hailsham once did to the late Lord Birkett.[3] Nevertheless it is hard to see how the discovery of the truth and the protection of the innocent from unjust conviction can be regarded as alternative objectives: the more accurately the relevant facts are established the less the probability that a wrongful conviction will result. When, however, the facts are in doubt the price that must be paid for safeguarding the innocent is the risk that the guilty will go free; and the greater the doubt the higher this price will be.

---

[2] Viscount Dilhorne, House of Lords Official Report, May 8, 1963, col. 712.

[3] House of Lords Official Report, February 8, 1962, col. 342.

Even within its own terms of reference, however, the process of trial might, perhaps, benefit from a little modernisation. No one can fail to be struck by the contrast between the high degree of sophistication attained by forensic science in the detection of crime, and the pre-scientific character of the criminal process itself—between the skill and zeal with which modern scientific methods are seized upon in order to bring an offender to justice, and the neglect of such methods in what happens when he gets there. Consider for a moment some of the familiar aspects of a criminal trial. In order to arrive at a verdict it is necessary to disentangle the truth about past events from conflicting, incomplete, distorted and often deliberately falsified accounts. At the best of times and in the best of hands this is bound to be an extremely difficult matter. Many psychological experiments have demonstrated the unreliability of the ordinary person's recollection of previous happenings, even in circumstances in which every effort is made to achieve accuracy and in which there can be no motive for falsification. Yet in our criminal courts in the vast majority of cases, including those of the utmost gravity, this task devolves upon completely inexperienced juries or upon amateur magistrates; and in the case of juries, upon whom the heaviest responsibility rests, the sacred secrecy of the jury room precludes any investigation into the methods by which, or the efficiency with which, they discharge their task. Nor do these amateurs even enjoy the help of modern technical devices. Without benefit of tape-recorder or transcription, juries are not even furnished with elementary facilities for taking notes. The facts upon which their verdict should be based are recorded only in their memory of the witnesses' memory of the original events: or in their memory of the judge's summing-up of the witnesses' memory of the original events. Indeed in the use of modern recording instruments our courts are almost unbelievably antiquated. To this day[4] in London magistrates' courts evidence is

[4] See Postscript to this chapter for the situation 17 years later.

written down by the clerk in longhand—a procedure which I have never found paralleled, although I have visited similar courts in the United States, Canada, Australia, India, Japan and Ghana, as well as in Europe.

Some of these inadequacies are inevitable. Trials cannot be held on the spot, and memories are bound to fade. Trivial events which later prove to be of vital significance are bound to be overlooked at the time or imperfectly recollected. But even so, something could I think be done to improve the criminal process as a method of historical investigation. Juries might be supplied with transcriptions of the evidence—or better still with tape-recordings, since it is not only what a witness says, but how he says it, which is important; or, at the very least, a recording should be available in the jury room of the judge's summing-up, for this alone in an important case can be long enough to impose a serious tax on memory: it has been known to last 10 hours. Admittedly such changes would add to the cost of trials; but hardly in proportion to the risk of convictions or acquittals not justified by the facts.

Memories, too, might be greener if the interval between the commission of an offence and the trial of the person charged were kept to a minimum. So far as the period between committal and trial is concerned, the Criminal Justice Administration Act of 1962, following on the recommendations of the Streatfeild Committee, should now[5] make it possible for the interval between committal and trial never to exceed eight weeks, and normally to approximate to the four-week period which is already usual at the Old Bailey and such other courts as are in more or less continuous session. These improvements, however, relate only to the lapse of time between committal proceedings and subsequent trial, and do nothing to mitigate the long delays which sometimes occur before a prosecution is initiated. Even if such delays are sometimes unavoidable

[5] This hope has alas, not been realised: in the late seventies delays have often been very much longer.

in serious charges, where evidence can often only be collected with difficulty and over a considerable period of time, this does not explain the long interval that often elapses—in London at any rate—particularly in motoring cases, between the commission of an offence and the resulting proceedings in the magistrates' court. At the best of times evidence in traffic cases is apt to be singularly elusive; but the supposition that speeds and distances and traffic conditions in a single incident on the road can be accurately recollected six, seven or eight months later can only be described as farcical.

Better recording and quicker trials would certainly do something to improve the efficiency of fact-finding in the criminal courts. Is it impertinent for a layman to suggest that changes in the conventions of advocacy might do more? In spite of the extreme conservatism of the legal profession, these conventions need not be regarded as wholly immutable. Indeed they are subtly changing all the time. The extravagant and often irrelevant oratory of an earlier age, for instance, has today given way to a more sober style, and the highly emotional approach of a generation or two ago sounds very oddly in contemporary ears. So it is not unreasonable to hope for further changes. In particular one could wish to see less readiness to pose unanswerable questions. Justice is not promoted by asking a witness, as I have heard a witness asked, why he did not see the trafficator on a vehicle which he has already said he did not see at all; nor by pressing a cyclist who was thrown into the air by collision with a motorcycle to state exactly on what part of his machine the impact occurred. Too often, also, inferences from shaky premises become clothed with an air of spurious certainty, as when elaborate and convincing explanations are based on the behaviour of a hypothetical person whose presence nobody can confidently remember, but equally no one can categorically deny. By the time that counsel has finished, this hypothetical figure has become so real that the court can almost picture what he was wearing; and, most sinister of all, the witness who first cast doubt upon his existence is now wholly convinced of his reality. Truth would be better served if professional etiquette could be extended to require that the distinction between the hypothetical and the agreed (between "he could have been there" and "he was there") must not be blurred. Witnesses, too, ought surely to be more explicitly encouraged to admit the limitations of their own memory or observation; and to appreciate that, understandable as is their reluctance continually to repeat "I do not know" or "I do not remember," there is nothing discreditable in so doing. Particularly is this true in the many cases in which the minutiae of time or space are important. Judges, magistrates and lawyers might indeed do well to study more closely the known facts of the psychology of perception, and to take to heart Professor Vernon's warning that "experiments indicate that it is not possible to perceive and attend to two events separately and independently if these coincide too nearly in time or space. Either one will cancel out the other or they will be combined in some way if this is at all possible."[6]

In other words, even within an accusatorial procedure, more weight might be given on both sides to the ascertainment of fact. After all, in England at any rate, a criminal trial is not a free-for-all. The prosecutor at least operates within many conventional restraints: he does not, as in some other countries, clamour for the imposition of a particular penalty; and he is often scrupulously fair in exposing the weaknesses in his own case. Is it so certain that the interests of justice or even the interests of defendants are served by the gross distortions of fact and indeed the unmitigated nonsense which is often advanced by defending counsel? For my part I could wish—and I suspect that many experienced magistrates would say the same—that the whole question of the conventions of

---

[6] Vernon, M. D., *The Psychology of Perception* (Penguin Books) 1962, p. 171.

defence advocacy, and even more of the efficiency of present criminal procedure as a means of arriving at the truth, might be examined by the Bar.[7] The moment for such suggestions seems moreover to be opportune, for the profession appears to be in a remarkably receptive mood. Within two days of each other, first the Attorney-General is reported to have reminded the Bar Council that "the public could have no confidence in any profession unless it were alert frequently to review its practices and to see that they corresponded to the requirements of the modern age,"[8] and, second, the Lord Chancellor is said to have suggested at the judges' Mansion House dinner that the wind of change must be felt in the corridors of the courts "if we, in the law, are to keep abreast of the times."[9]

Proposals for the modernisation of the methods by which the criminal courts arrive at their verdicts do not, however, attempt to answer any question as to the object of the whole exercise. Much more fundamental are the issues which arise after conviction, when many a judge or magistrate must from time to time have asked himself just what it is that he is trying to achieve. Is he trying to punish the wicked, or to prevent the recurrence of forbidden acts? The former is certainly the traditional answer and is still deeply entrenched both in the legal profession and in the minds of much of the public at large; and it has been reasserted in uncompromising terms by a former Lord Chief Justice. At a meeting of magistrates in 1963 Lord Goddard is reported to have said that the duty of the criminal law was to punish—and that reformation of the prisoner was not the courts' business.[10] Those who take this view doubtless comfort themselves with the belief that

[7] Or better still by an independent body, such as the Royal Commission on Criminal Procedure, whose Report is expected just as this edition goes to print.

[8] *The Times*, July 16, 1963.

[9] *The Times*, July 18, 1963.

[10] *The Observer*, May 5, 1963.

the two objectives are nearly identical: that the punishment of the wicked is also the best way to prevent the occurrence of prohibited acts. Yet the continual failure of a mainly punitive system to diminish the volume of crime strongly suggests that such comfort is illusory; and it will indeed be a principal theme of these lectures that the choice between the punitive and the preventive[11] concept of the criminal process is a real one; and that, according as that choice is made, radical differences must follow in the courts' approach to their task. I shall, moreover, argue that in recent years a perceptible shift has occurred away from the first and towards the second of these two conceptions of the function of the criminal law; and that this movement is greatly to be welcomed and might with advantage be both more openly acknowledged and also accelerated.[12]

First, however, let us examine the implications of the traditional view. Presumably the wickedness which renders a criminal liable to punishment must be inherent either in the actions which he has committed or in the state of mind in which he has committed them. Can we then in the modern world identify a class of inherently wicked actions? Lord Devlin, who has returned more than once to this theme, holds that we still can, by drawing a sharp distinction between what he calls the criminal and the quasi-criminal law. The distinguishing mark of the latter, in his view, is that a breach of it does not mean that the offender has done anything morally wrong. "Real" crimes, on the other hand, he describes as "sins with legal definitions"; and he adds that "It is a pity that this distinction, which I believe the ordinary man readily recognises, is not acknowledged in the administration of justice." "The sense of

---

[11] I use this word throughout to describe a system the primary purpose of which is to prevent the occurrence of offences, whether committed by persons already convicted or by other people. The relative importance of these two ("special" and "general") aspects of prevention is discussed in Chap. 4 below. See pp. 96 *et seq.*

[12] But for signs of a counter-reaction see Postscript to this Chapter, pp. 60 ff.

obligation which leads the citizen to obey a law that is good in itself is," he says, "different in quality from that which leads to obedience to a regulation designed to secure a good end." Nor does his Lordship see any reason "why the quasi-criminal should be treated with any more ignominy than a man who has incurred a penalty for failing to return a library book in time."[13] And in a personal communication he has further defined the "real" criminal law as any part of the criminal law, new or old, which the good citizen does not break without a sense of guilt.

Nevertheless this attempt to revive the lawyer's distinction between *mala in se* and *mala prohibita*—things which are bad in themselves and things which are merely prohibited—cannot, I think, succeed. In the first place the statement that a real crime is one about which the good citizen would feel guilty is surely circular. For how is the good citizen to be defined in this context unless as one who feels guilty about committing the crimes that Lord Devlin classifies as "real"? And in the second place the badness even of those actions which would most generally be regarded as *mala in se* is inherent, not in the physical acts themselves, but in the circumstances in which they are performed. Indeed it is hard to think of any examples of actions which could, in a strictly physical sense, be said to be bad in themselves. The physical act of stealing merely involves moving a piece of matter from one place to another: what gives it its immoral character is the framework of property rights in which it occurs. Only the violation of these rights transforms an inherently harmless movement into the iniquitous act of stealing. Nor can bodily assaults be unequivocally classified as *mala in se*; for actions which in other circumstances would amount to grievous bodily harm may be not only legal, but highly beneficial, when performed by competent surgeons; and

[13] Devlin, Sir Patrick (now Lord), *Law and Morals* (University of Birmingham, 1961), pp. 3, 7, 8, 9.

there are those who see no wrong in killing in the form of judicial hanging or in war.

One is indeed tempted to suspect that actions classified as *mala in se* are really only *mala antiqua*—actions, that is to say, which have been recognised as criminal for a very long time; and that the tendency to dismiss sundry modern offences as "merely quasi-crimes" is simply a mark of not having caught up with the realities of the contemporary world. The criminal calendar is always the expression of a particular social and moral climate, and from one generation to another it is modified by two sets of influences. On the one hand ideas about what is thought to be right or wrong are themselves subject to change; and on the other hand new technical developments constantly create new opportunities for anti-social actions which the criminal code must be extended to include. To a thorough-going Marxist these two types of change would not, presumably, be regarded as mutually independent: to the Marxist it is technical innovations which cause moral judgments to be revised. But for present purposes it does not greatly matter whether the one is, or is not, the cause of the other. In either case the technical and the moral are distinguishable. The fact that there is nothing in the Ten Commandments about the iniquity of driving a motor-vehicle under the influence of drink cannot be read as evidence that the ancient Israelites regarded this offence more leniently than the contemporary British. On the other hand the divergent attitudes of our own criminal law and that of most European countries to homosexual practices has no obvious relation to technical development, and is clearly the expression of differing moral judgments, or at the least to different conceptions of the proper relation between morality and the criminal law.

One has only to glance, too, at the maximum penalties which the law has attached to various offences to realise how profoundly attitudes change in course of time. Life imprisonment, for example, was within living memory not the only obligatory sentence for murder and the maximum permissible for manslaughter. It could also be imposed for blasphemy or for the destruction of registers of births or baptisms. Again, the crime of abducting an heiress carried a potential sentence of 14 years, while that for the abduction of a child under 14 years was only half as long. For administering a drug to a female with a view to carnal knowledge a maximum of two years was provided, but for damage to cattle you were liable to fourteen years' imprisonment. For using unlawful oaths the maximum was seven years, but for keeping a child in a brothel a mere six months. Such sentences strike us today as quite fantastic; but they cannot have seemed fantastic to those who devised them. Periodical revisions have, however, removed most of these anachronisms and will no doubt deal likewise with others as the climate of opinion changes.

For the origins of the supposed dichotomy between real crimes and quasi-crimes we must undoubtedly look to theology, as Lord Devlin's use of the term "sins with legal definitions" itself implies. The links between law and religion are both strong and ancient. Indeed, as Lord Radcliffe has lately reminded us, it has taken centuries for "English judges to realise that the tenets and injunctions of the Christian religion were not part of the common law of England"[14]; and even today such realisation does not seem to be complete. As recently as 1961, in the "Ladies Directory" case, the defendant Shaw, you may remember, was convicted of conspiring to corrupt public morals, as well as of offences against the Sexual Offences Act of 1956 and the Obscene Publications Act of 1959, on account of his publication of a directory in which the ladies of the town advertised their services, sometimes, it would seem, in considerable detail. In rejecting Shaw's appeal to the House of Lords on the charge of conspiracy, Lord Simonds delivered himself of the opinion that without doubt "there remains in the courts a residual power

[14] Radcliffe, Lord, *The Law and Its Compass* (Faber, 1961), p. 12.

to . . . conserve not only the safety but also the moral welfare of the state"; and Lord Hodson, concurring, added that "even if Christianity be not part of the law of England, yet the common law has its roots in Christianity."[1 5]

In the secular climate of the present age, however, the appeal to religious doctrine is unconvincing, and unlikely to be generally acceptable. Instead we must recognise a range of actions, the badness of which is inherent not in themselves, but in the circumstances in which they are performed, and which stretches in a continuous scale from wilful murder at one end to failure to observe a no-parking rule or to return on time a library book (which someone else may be urgently wanting) at the other. (Incidentally a certain poignancy is given to Lord Devlin's choice of this last example by a subsequent newspaper report that a book borrower in Frankfurt who omitted, in spite of repeated requests, to return a book which he had borrowed two years previously was brought before a local magistrate actually—though apparently by mistake—in handcuffs.[1 6]) But however great the range from the heinous to the trivial, the important point is that the gradation is continuous; and in the complexities of modern society a vast range of actions, in themselves apparently morally neutral, must be regarded as in varying degrees anti-social, and therefore in their contemporary settings as no less objectionable than actions whose criminal status is of greater antiquity. The good citizen will doubtless experience different degrees of guilt according as he may have stabbed his wife, engaged in homosexual intercourse with a school boy, omitted to return his library book or failed to prevent one of his employees from watering the milk sold by his firm. Technically these are all crimes; whether or not they are also sins is a purely theological matter with which the law has no concern. If the function of the criminal law is to punish the wicked, then every-

---

[1 5] *Shaw* v. *Director of Public Prosecutions* [1961] 2 W.L.R. 897.
[1 6] *The Times*, November 11, 1961.

thing which the law forbids must in the circumstances in which it is forbidden be regarded as in its appropriate measure wicked.

Although this is, I think, the inevitable conclusion of any argument which finds wickedness inherent in particular classes of action, it seems to be unpalatable to Lord Devlin and others who nevertheless conceive the function of the criminal law in punitive terms. It opens the door too wide. Still, the door can be closed again by resort to the alternative theory that the wickedness of an action is inherent not in the action itself, but in the state of mind of the person who performs it. To punish people merely for what they have done, it is argued, would be unjust, for the forbidden act might have been an accident for which the person who did it cannot be held to blame. Hence the requirement, to which traditionally the law attaches so much importance, that a crime is not, so to speak, a crime in the absence of *mens rea*.

Today, however, over a wide front even this requirement has in fact been abandoned. Today many, indeed probably the majority, of the cases dealt with by the criminal courts are cases of strict liability in which proof of a guilty mind is no longer necessary for conviction. A new dichotomy is thus created, and one which in this instance exists not merely in the minds of the judges but is actually enshrined in the law itself—that is to say, the dichotomy between those offences in which the guilty mind is, and those in which it is not, an essential ingredient. In large measure, no doubt, this classification coincides with Lord Devlin's division into real and quasi-crimes; but whether or not this coincidence is exact must be a question of personal judgment. To drive a car when your driving ability is impaired through drink or drugs is an offence of strict liability: it is no defence to say that you had no idea that the drink would affect you as it did, or to produce evidence that you were such a seasoned drinker that any such result was, objectively, not to be expected. These might be mitigating circumstances after conviction, but are no bar to the conviction itself. Yet some at least of those who distinguish between real and quasi-crimes would put drunken driving in the former category, even when it involves no question of *mens rea*. In the passage that I quoted earlier Lord Devlin, it will be remembered, was careful to include new as well as old offences in his category of "real" crimes; but generally speaking it is the *mala antiqua* which are held to be both *mala in se* and contingent upon *mens rea*.

Nothing has dealt so devastating a blow at the punitive conception of the criminal process as the proliferation of offences of strict liability; and the alarm has forthwith been raised. Thus Dr. J. Ll. J. Edwards has expressed the fear that there is a real danger that the "widespread practice of imposing criminal liability independent of any moral fault" will result in the criminal law being regarded with contempt. "The process of basing criminal liability upon a theory of absolute prohibition," he writes, "may well have the opposite effect to that intended and lead to a weakening of respect for the law."[17] Nor, in his view, is it an adequate answer to say that absolute liability can be tolerated because of the comparative unimportance of the offences to which it is applied and because, as a rule, only a monetary penalty is involved; for, in the first place, there are a number of important exceptions to this rule (drunken driving for example); and, secondly, as Dr. Edwards himself points out, in certain cases the penalty imposed by the court may be the least part of the punishment. A merchant's conviction for a minor trading offence may have a disastrous effect upon his business.

Such dislike of strict liability is not by any means confined to academic lawyers. In the courts, too, various devices have been used to smuggle *mens rea* back into offences from which, on the face of it, it would appear to be excluded. To the lawyer's ingenious mind the invention

[17] Edwards, J. Ll. J., *Mens Rea in Statutory Offences* (Macmillan, 1955), p. 247.

of such devices naturally presents no difficulty. Criminal liability, for instance, can attach only to voluntary acts. If a driver is struck unconscious with an epileptic seizure, it can be argued that he is not responsible for any consequences because his driving thereafter is involuntary: indeed he has been said not to be driving at all. If on the other hand he falls asleep, this defence will not serve since sleep is a condition that comes on gradually, and a driver has an opportunity and a duty to stop before it overpowers him. Alternatively, recourse can be had to the circular argument that anyone who commits a forbidden act must have intended to commit it and must, therefore, have formed a guilty intention. As Lord Devlin puts it, the word "knowingly" or "wilfully" can be read into acts in which it is not present; although, as his Lordship points out, this subterfuge is open to the criticism that it fails to distinguish between the physical act itself and the circumstances in which this becomes a crime.[18] All that the accused may have intended was to perform an action (such as firing a gun or driving a car) which is not in itself criminal. Again, in yet other cases such as those in which it is forbidden to permit or to allow something to be done, the concept of negligence can do duty as a watered down version of *mens rea*: for how can anyone be blamed for permitting something about which he could not have known?

All these devices, it cannot be too strongly emphasised, are necessitated by the need to preserve the essentially punitive function of the criminal law. For it is not, as Dr. Edwards fears, the criminal law which will be brought into contempt by the multiplication of offences of strict liability, so much as this particular conception of the law's function. If that function is conceived less in terms of punishment than as a mechanism of prevention, these fears become irrelevant. Such a conception, however, apparently sticks in the throat of even the most progressive lawyers. Even Professor Hart, in his Hobhouse lecture on *Punish-*

---

[18] Devlin, Lord, *Samples of Law Making* (O.U.P., 1962), pp. 71-80.

ment and the Elimination of Responsibility, [19] seems to be
incurably obsessed with the notion of punishment, which
haunts his text as well as figuring in his title. Although
rejecting many traditional theories, such as that punishment should be "retributive" or "denunciatory," he nevertheless seems wholly unable to envisage a system in which
sentence is not automatically equated with "punishment."
Thus he writes of "values quite distinct from those of
retributive punishment which the system of responsibility
does maintain, and which remain of great importance even
if our aims in *punishing*[20] are the forward-looking aims of
social protection"; and again "even if we *punish* men not
as wicked but as nuisances . . ." while he makes many
references to the principle that liability to punishment
must depend on a voluntary act. Perhaps it requires the
naivete of an amateur to suggest that the forward-looking
aims of social protection might, on occasion, have absolutely
no connection with punishment.

If, however, the primary function of the courts is conceived as the prevention of forbidden acts, there is little
cause to be disturbed by the multiplication of offences of
strict liability. If the law says that certain things are not to
be done, it is illogical to confine this prohibition to
occasions on which they are done from malice aforethought;
for at least the material consequences of an action, and the
reasons for prohibiting it, are the same whether it is the
result of sinister malicious plotting, of negligence or of
sheer accident. A man is equally dead and his relatives
equally bereaved whether he was stabbed or run over by a
drunken motorist or by an incompetent one; and the
inconvenience caused by the loss of your bicycle is
unaffected by the question whether or not the youth who
removed it had the intention of putting it back, if in fact
he had not done so at the time of his arrest. It is true, of

---

[19] Hart, H. L. A., *Punishment and the Elimination of Responsibility*
(Athlone Press, 1962), pp. 27, 28.
[20] Italics added.

course, as Professor Hart has argued,[21] that the material consequences of an action by no means exhaust its effects. "If one person hits another, the person struck does not think of the other as *just* a cause of pain to him . . . If the blow was light but deliberate, it has a significance for the person struck quite different from an accidental much heavier blow." To ignore this difference, he argues, is to outrage "distinctions which not only underlie morality, but pervade the whole of our social life." That these distinctions are widely appreciated and keenly felt no one would deny. Often perhaps they derive their force from a purely punitive or retributive attitude; but alternatively they may be held to be relevant to an assessment of the social damage that results from a criminal act. Just as a heavy blow does more damage than a light one, so also perhaps does a blow which involves psychological injury do more damage than one in which the hurt is purely physical.

The conclusion to which this argument leads is, I think, not that the presence or absence of the guilty mind is unimportant, but that *mens rea* has, so to speak—and this is the crux of the matter—*got into the wrong place.* Traditionally, the requirement of the guilty mind is written into the actual definition of a crime. No guilty intention, no crime, is the rule. Obviously this makes sense if the law's concern is with wickedness: where there is no guilty intention, there can be no wickedness. But it is equally obvious, on the other hand, that an action does not become innocuous merely because whoever performed it meant no harm. If the object of the criminal law is to prevent the occurrence of socially damaging actions, it would be absurd to turn a blind eye to those which were due to carelessness, negligence or even accident. The question of motivation is *in the first instance* irrelevant.

But only in the first instance. At a later stage, that is to say, after what is now known as a conviction, the presence

[21] *Op. cit.,* pp. 29, 30.

or absence of guilty intention is all-important for its effect on the appropriate measures to be taken to prevent a recurrence of the forbidden act. The prevention of accidental deaths presents different problems from those involved in the prevention of wilful murders. The results of the actions of the careless, the mistaken, the wicked and the merely unfortunate may be indistinguishable from one another, but each case calls for a different treatment. Tradition, however, is very strong, and the notion that these differences are relevant only after the fact has been established that the accused committed the forbidden act seems still to be deeply abhorrent to the legal mind. Thus Lord Devlin, discussing the possibility that judges might have taken the line that all "unintentional" criminals might be dealt with simply by the imposition of a nominal penalty, regards this as the "negation of law." "It would,"[22] he says,

> "confuse the function of mercy which the judge is dispensing when imposing the penalty with the function of justice. It would have been to deny to the citizen due process of law because it would have been to say to him, in effect: 'Although we cannot think that Parliament intended you to be punished in this case because you have really done nothing wrong, come to us, ask for mercy, and we shall grant mercy.' . . . In all criminal matters the citizen is entitled to protection of the law . . . and the mitigation of penalty should not be adopted as the prime method of dealing with accidental offenders."

Within its own implied terms of reference the logic is unexceptionable. If the purpose of the law is to dispense punishment tempered with mercy, then to use mercy as a consolation for unjust punishment is certainly to give a stone for bread. But these are not the implied terms of reference of strict liability. In the case of offences of strict liability the presumption is not that those who have

[22] Devlin, Lord, *Samples of Law Making* (O.U.P., 1962), p. 73.

committed forbidden actions must be punished, but that appropriate steps must be taken to prevent the occurrence of such actions.

Here, as often in other contexts also, the principles involved are admirably illustrated by the many driving offences in which conviction does not involve proof of *mens rea*. If, for instance, the criterion of gravity is the amount of social damage which a crime causes, many of these offences must be judged extremely grave. In 1961 299 persons were convicted on charges of causing death by dangerous driving, that is to say more than five times as many as were convicted of murder (including those found guilty but insane) and 85 per cent. more than the total of convictions for all other forms of homicide (namely murder, manslaughter and infanticide) put together. It is, moreover, a peculiarity of many driving offences that the offender seldom intends the actual damage which he causes. He may be to blame in that he takes a risk which he knows may result in injury to other people or to their property, but such injury is neither an inevitable nor an intended consequence of the commission of the offence: which is not true of, for example, burglary. Dangerous or careless driving ranges in a continuous series from the almost wholly accidental, through the incompetent and the negligent to the positively and grossly culpable; and it is quite exceptionally difficult in many of these cases to establish just to what point along this scale any particular instance should be assigned. In consequence the gravity of any offence tends to be estimated by its consequences rather than by the state of mind of the perpetrator—which is less usual (although attempted murder or grievous bodily harm may turn into murder, if the victim dies) in the case of other crimes. In my experience it is exceptional (though not unknown) for a driving charge to be made unless an accident actually occurs, and the nature of the charge is apt to be determined by the severity of the accident. I recall, for example, a case in which a car driver knocked down an elderly man on a pedestrian crossing, and a month later the victim died in hospital after an operation, his death being, one must suppose, in spite, rather than because, of this. Thereupon the charge, which had originally been booked by the police as careless, not even dangerous, driving was upgraded to causing death by dangerous driving.

For all these reasons it is recognised that there are many offences which, if they are to be dealt with by the criminal courts at all, can only be judged on a basis of strict liability. Motoring offences in particular illustrate all too vividly the fact that in the modern world in one way or another, as much and more damage is done by negligence, or by indifference to the welfare or safety of others, as by deliberate wickedness. In technically simpler societies this is less likely to be so, for the points of exposure to the follies of others are less numerous, and the daily chances of being run over, or burnt or infected or drowned because someone has left undone something that he ought to have done are less ominous. These new complexities were never envisaged by the founders of our legal traditions, and it is hardly to be wondered at if the law itself is not yet fully adapted to them. Yet it is by no means certain that the last chapter in the long and chequered history of the concept of guilt, which is so deeply rooted in our traditions, has yet been written. Time was when inanimate objects—the rock that fell on you, the tree that attracted the lightning that killed you—were held to share the blame for the disasters in which they were instrumental; and it was properly regarded as a great step forward when the capacity to acquire a guilty mind was deemed to be one of the distinctive capacities of human beings.[2][3] But now, perhaps, the time has come for the concept of legal guilt to be dissolved into a wider concept of responsibility or at least accountability, in which there is room for negligence as

---

[2][3] There could be an argument here, into which I do not propose to enter, as to whether this capacity is not shared by some of the higher animals.

well as purposeful wrong doing; and for the significance of
a conviction to be reinterpreted merely as evidence that a
prohibited act has been committed, questions of motivation
being relevant only in so far as they bear upon the
probability of such acts being repeated.

I am not, of course, arguing that all crimes should
immediately be transferred into the strict liability category.
To do so would in some cases involve formidable problems
of definition—as, for instance, in that of theft. But I do
suggest that the contemporary extension of strict liability
is not the nightmare that it is often made out to be, that it
does not promise the decline and fall of the criminal law,
and that it is, on the contrary, a sensible and indeed
inevitable measure of adaptation to the requirements of
the modern world; and above all I suggest that its supposedly
nightmarish quality disappears once it is accepted that the
primary objective of the criminal courts is preventive
rather than punitive. Certainly we need to pay heed to
Professor Walker's reminder[24] that "under our present law
it is possible for a person to do great harm in circumstances
which suggest that there is a risk of his repeating it, and
yet to secure an acquittal." In two types of case, in both
of which such harm can result, the concept of the guilty
mind has become both irrelevant and obstructive. In this
lecture I have been chiefly concerned with the first of these
categories—that of cases of negligence. The second
category—that of mental abnormality—will be the theme
of that which follows.

[24] Walker, Professor N., "Queen Victoria Was Right," *New Society*,
June 27, 1963.

In the past 16 year there has been a spate of legislation and procedural changes relating to the powers and practice of the courts at all levels. To begin with the minor, purely mechanical, matters mentioned in my lecture, materials for taking notes are now supposed to be available for all juries, but even in London they are only issued as requested, and we are as far away as ever from jurors being able to listen in the jury room to repeats of recorded evidence which they may have heard several days, if not weeks, earlier. In magistrates' courts, at least in London, but certainly not throughout the country, it is officially said that clerks were issued with dictaphones some years ago, but it remains a matter for each clerk to decide whether or not to use this equipment, in preference to his own long- or short-hand. Some have reverted to the latter, because of difficulty in getting transcriptions rapidly enough for repetition to the Bench.

The great majority of magistrates are still "amateurs" but they are no longer "untrained." Attendance at a (not always very arduous) training course is now obligatory throughout the country before a lay magistrate is permitted to adjudicate in court. Moreover in 1976 the then Lord Chancellor and the Home Office in a moment of great daring jointly appointed a Working Party to review the whole question of Judicial Training, which would have included training of the professional, as well as the amateur, judiciary. That revolutionary proposal, however, soon foundered on the convenient obstacle of expense. But at least it has now become customary for judges to arrange sentencing conferences among themselves.

At the time of my lectures, both judges and magistrates were permitted to sit in courts till death did them part, but today judicial personnel at all levels are subject to compulsory retirement at various ages ranging from 70 to 75. Thus lay magistrates must all retire at 70, stipendiaries also at 70, but with possible extension to 72, circuit judges at 72, extensible to 75, and High Court judges (if appointed since 1959) at 75. Apparently the underlying principle is that the risks of senility vary inversely with the elevation of the post occupied.

The Criminal Justice Act of 1967 was a landmark in the development of the contemporary penal system. Among its many changes was the introduction of a simplified procedure for magistrates' committal of defendants for trial, by which the accused may be committed purely on written statements submitted by the prosecution (which the magistrates need not even read), provided that he is legally represented, and that the defence has not submitted that these statements contain insufficient evidence to justify committal. This procedure undoubtedly saves time and money, and, coupled with the prohibition on publicising committal proceedings (except when this is expressly requested by the accused), it probably increases the chance of a fair trial; but I doubt if it has made much difference to anyone's chance of being sent, or not sent, for trial, since, in my 40-odd years in magistrates' courts prior to this change, I can only think of one case in which we refused to commit. From the magistrates' point of view, however, it has meant loss of opportunities to become acquainted with much material that is both criminologically and humanly interesting. Certainly my own eyes were opened to the international ramifications of certain kinds of criminality on hearing the prosecution evidence in committal proceedings against a Cypriot woman charged with abortion, whose name had apparently been given by someone in Denmark to an Englishman who had allegedly made an Irish girl pregnant in London.

But of all the procedural changes for which the 1967 Act was responsible, probably the most radical was the legalisation of majority verdicts by juries (provided that there is not more than one dissentient where there are 10 jurors or two where there are 11 or 12). A similar rule has long been operative in Scotland, where according to Lord Boothby[1] it has worked very well. Since, however, no data exist on which to assess how many persons in Scotland have been convicted by a majority verdict, who would have been acquitted had a unanimous vote been necessary or *vice versa*, his Lordship's judgement cannot be founded on any solid evidence. Myself I am inclined to see the change as one of several signs of a contemporary movement to make convictions easier.

Of course juries are not infallible. That has been repeatedly confirmed by researches in both the United States of America and this country[2] in which a "shadow" jury, drawn from persons who might have been called to serve as jurors in a particular case have listened to the proceedings throughout in the public gallery and then arrived at their own verdict by private discussion in the same way as did the real jury. In a significant minority of such cases the shadow and the actual verdicts have not coincided, so whichever way the case went, a reasonable doubt must be presumed.

For the democratisation of the jury system we had to wait until the Criminal Justice Act of 1972, when the property qualification for jurors was abolished and the minimum age of service reduced to 18, so that in effect the qualifications for jury service and for the right to vote are now the same, except that certain professions (*e.g.* police or magistrates) are exempt from jury service and there is an age limit at 60. The 1967 Act also disqualified for 10 years persons who had served a sentence of over 3 months, and for life anyone who had ever been imprisoned for over 5 years.

More recently there has been considerable discussion of "jury vetting" - another sign of the movement to secure

---

[1] House of Lords Official Report, May 10, 1967, col. 1477.

[2] See, for example, McCabe, Sarah and Purves, Robert, *The Shadow Jury at Work* (Blackwell, 1974).

convictions more readily. The upshot has been a decision by the Court of Appeal in June 1980 that prosecuting counsel in criminal cases could be given access to jurors' criminal records, even though a criminal record (except as prescribed by the above mentioned provisions of the 1967 Act) is not in itself a bar to jury service.

In the past two decades the powers of the courts in relation to their second function - that of deciding how to deal with persons found guilty - have been both restricted and extended. Most notable among the restrictions was the abolition in 1965 of capital punishment as the mandatory sentence for murder, and the substitution of an (also mandatory) life sentence, with the judge having power to make a (not legally binding) recommendation as to the minimum period that the prisoner should serve before being released on licence. The 1967 Act also put an end to corporal punishment in prisons, and abolished the sentences of "corrective training" (which in practice had never meant much more than ordinary imprisonment) and of "preventive detention"; but in place of the latter, a new sentence of "extended imprisonment" was substituted, under which a persistent offender could be sentenced to a term of imprisonment additional to the maximum for the offence for which he was currently before the court. This latest version of the long story of attempts to impose special conditions on persistent offenders has however already become virtually a dead letter.

The extensions of the courts' sentencing powers included first, the introduction (again under the 1967 Act) of the power to suspend prison sentences so that these only come into effect if the offender is further convicted of an "imprisonable" offence within a specified period (originally three years, but reduced in 1972 to two). Activation of the suspended sentence is not however mandatory, if the court dealing with the new offence thinks that, in all the circumstances at the time, the double sentence would be unjust. Considerable use has been made by the courts of the power to suspend, some 35,000 sentences being suspended in 1978; and in the same year some 10,000 persons (three-quarters of whom were immediately imprisoned) were convicted of breaches of an order previously imposing a suspended sentence. When the principle of suspension was first introduced, it was hoped that it would reduce overcrowding in prisons; but expert statistical opinions differ as to whether in fact it has done so, or whether it may not have had the reverse effect.

Under the Criminal Justice Act of 1972 the armoury of the courts was enlarged by the addition of two new sentences,[3] both as the result of recommendations by the Advisory Council on the Penal System. First was the power to impose Criminal Bankruptcy orders as a method of making successful thieves and robbers disgorge their ill-gotten gains; but this applies only to sums over £15,000 and has not been extensively used. In 1978 only 53 Criminal Bankruptcy Orders were made by the Crown Court.

The second new sentence, also introduced on the recommendation of the Penal Advisory Council, was the Community Service Order. This was originally made available only in half-a-dozen experimental areas, but can now be imposed by any court throughout England and Wales and has since been extended by separate legislation to Scotland. Under a C.S. Order an offender can be required to undertake a form of community service in his spare time, as prescribed by the court (with the advice of specially qualified probation officers). The service must occupy not less than 40 or more than 240 hours spread over a period of not more than 12 months. In practice the forms of service have been extremely varied, ranging from clearing neglected canals to helping in institutions for mentally retarded children, decorating elderly people's homes or working in their gardens. Occasionally much

---

[3] Penal Advisory Council, *Report on Reparation by the Offender* (H.M.S.O., 1970) and *Report on Non-Custodial and Semi-Custodial Penalties* (H.M.S.O., 1970).

ingenuity has been shown in fitting the form of service required to the particular individual concerned - as when an elderly woman shoplifter who was a good pianist was directed to spend her evenings playing the piano in an old people's home. As with probation orders, the offender's consent to a C.S. Order is necessary, partly because an objector would be unlikely to give much useful service, and partly because there is a possibility that compulsory work might be held to violate international conventions against slavery.

The number of persons annually made subject to C.S. Orders in England and Wales rose from 1,000 in 1974 to nearly 14,000 in 1978, and by the end of that year the total of Orders imposed over these five years had reached 37,900. It is also encouraging that in the three years 1976, 1977 and 1978 the proportion of Orders "satisfactorily completed" was between 75 per cent. and 80 per cent. Nevertheless the general public and the media seem to be singularly unaware of the rapid development of this radical alternative to imprisonment. No official, or to my knowledge unofficial, research (apart from one investigation relating only to the six original experimental areas) has been undertaken into the subsequent recidivism of persons subject to C.S. Orders as compared with that of similar cases sentenced to imprisonment. However, even if the future history of the offender subject to a C.S. Order should prove to be no better than that of his counterpart sentenced to prison, at least we can be glad that C.S. is much cheaper than imprisonment, does not expose the offender to a "residential school for crime," and indeed while it lasts produces some useful result. Moreover it is known that in some cases persons whose orders have expired continue voluntarily at the tasks which they were previously under obligation to perform.

In addition to these new sentences, the powers of the courts have also been extended in two other ways. First the Criminal Justice Act of 1972 authorised a court to defer for a period of not more than six months passing sentence on a person, if his conduct or circumstances during that period would be likely to modify the choice of an appropriate sentence - a useful provision if, for example an offender offers to make reparation for any damage he has done, or if, though at the moment unemployed, he has an early prospect of getting a job.

Secondly, under the same Act a court now has power to insert a condition in a probation order requiring the probationer to attend a Day Training Centre for a period of up to 60 days: but in each of the three years since this provision was available it has been used in less than 200 cases, partly because there are only four such centres in the whole country, and partly because the obligation to attend regularly in the day-time virtually rules out most people in regular employment. Those centres that have been established seem, however, to have devised imaginative programmes dealing with practical matters, such as social security rights, or advice on how to apply for a job or to face an interview - some of which might with advantage be substituted for the more academic syllabuses used sometimes in educational courses in residential institutions for delinquents.

All these new provisions certainly amount to quite a substantial addition to the powers of judges and magistrates (both of whom can defer sentences, suspend imprisonment, impose a Community Service Order or require a probationer to attend a day training centre). Nevertheless the acquisition of a supply of new tools loses half its significance if their owners are not agreed as to the purpose to which they should be put. On one point, however, there has perhaps been agreement. All the changes that I have just listed are alternatives to imprisonment, and may have had a common objective as attempts to check the growth of the prison population, which, well before it had reached contemporary levels, was already regarded as a serious problem in the late sixties.

Nevertheless the conflict between the punitive and the reformative concepts of the function of the criminal law remains unresolved. Emphasis on the alleged distinction between actions which are *mala in se* and *mala prohibita* is increased by the attitude of both the public and the law to motoring offences, as illustrated by the examples quoted in my postscript to the previous lecture. While it is true that many of the - as they appear today - absurd penalties listed on page 41 have been brought more into line with modern assessments of the relative wickedness of various actions, that is merely a process of adapting the principle that the punishment should fit the crime to contemporary standards, as distinct from outright rejection of the primacy of a punitive, in favour of a reformative, objective.

For a time, reformist attitudes were greatly encouraged by yet another of the innovations introduced by the 1967 Act, namely, the establishment of a system of parole. In both Houses of Parliament this provision was received with considerable enthusiasm. The system itself is simple. Prisoners who have served at least a year or one-third of their sentences (whichever is the longer) become eligible for release on licence. If they wish to be considered for parole, they are interviewed by at least one member of a Local Review Committee (LRC) attached to the prison in which they are serving their sentence. In the case of the less serious offences this Committee may recommend release directly to the Home Secretary, whose decision is in all cases final. More serious cases are passed up by the LRC, with a favourable or unfavourable recommendation, to the Parole Board, a body appointed by the Home Secretary, with a membership which has ranged from time to time from under 20 to about 40 persons. By statute the members of the Board must include representatives of certain categories - such as psychiatrists, judges and criminologists - who might be expected to have appropriate knowledge or experience. The Board divides into panels of about half-a-dozen members who between them consider all the applications brought before it. Applicants are not interviewed by the Board or one of its panels, decisions being made on (often very voluminous) documentary evidence. Successful applicants are released under a standard form of licence which has a somewhat Victorian tone. This requires the subject to keep in touch with a designated officer of the probation and after-care service, to lead an industrious life and generally to be of good behaviour. Special conditions (*e.g.* as to residence or employment) may however be added in particular cases.

Early in its career, the Board made it abundantly clear where it stood on the question whether the duration of a sentence should be related to the iniquity of an offender's past conduct or to his probable future behaviour. Its 1972 Report observed that in cases where the balance between the interests of the prisoner and those of the community "is not clearly drawn, particularly where there appears to be substantial risk to the community, or where a release on parole may give rise to serious public anxiety, the Board's recommendations give first priority to the public interest".[4] In other words, the Board is more concerned with the prisoner's probable future than with his past. An elaborate "prediction table" has accordingly been devised showing, on the basis of past experience, the likely effect of some sixteen variables in a prisoner's life-story upon the prospect of his keeping out of trouble if released. The Home Office has, however, been at pains to emphasise that a candidate's "prediction score" is an aid to, not a substitute for, judgement.

The rosy dawn of the Parole Board did not, however, last long. Storms were soon brewing and criticisms blowing up, not least from ex-members of the Board itself. Among the latter were included such distinguished criminologists as Dr. D.J. West, J.E. Hall Williams and Roger Hood, all of whom went into print about the imperfections of the system of which they had had first-hand experience. Their criticisms related both to the fundamental philosophy of the Board and to various details of its practical operation, such as its failure to give unsuccessful candidates the

---

[4] Report of the Parole Board for 1972, para. 3.

reasons for their rejection, or the long delay between the time when a prisoner is eligible for parole and the date when his application is considered, and the further delay before a successful candidate is actually released.

Delays are of course administrative matters and could be dealt with by an increase in, or more efficient use of, available resources. The steady growth in the Board's membership should therefore make it possible to speed up the processing of applications by the simultaneous employment of more panels. As for the refusal to give reasons for rejection, it is noteworthy that Lord Hunt, the first Chairman of the Board has, since his retirement from that office, expressed the opinion that within the limits of administrative practicability, prisoners "have a moral right" to such explanations "which cannot be indefinitely denied".[5]

No doubt if and when applicants for parole are informed of the reasons why they are rejected, it will become highly desirable that this information should be accompanied by an opportunity to protest or to appeal. Roger Hood has accordingly proposed that the Parole Board should be transformed into a "judicial body with the authority of the High Court, appointed by the Lord Chancellor." But I for one am doubtful whether the average prisoner will greatly care whether his fate is decided by an executive or a judicial authority. If the decision goes against him, experience suggests that in either case he will be equally ready to ascribe prejudice or bias to its authors.

Critics also constantly deplore the embitterment of the disappointed; but against this must be set the relief of the successful. Of that much less (not surprisingly) is heard; but it is worth noting that the proportion of prisoners eligible for parole who receive it at some stage during their sentence had reached 60.1 per cent. by 1979, also that the average length of all licences granted in that year was eight months and that only 8.8 per cent. of parolees had to be recalled. In fact, thanks to parole a considerable number of ex-prisoners are at any one time at liberty in the community who would have otherwise still been in gaol.

But important though these issues are, the real gravamen of the charges brought against the Parole Board relates to its philosophy and objective, and particularly to its policy of looking to a prisoner's probable future behaviour, in preference to attempting an assessment of the iniquity of his past conduct. This policy has been denounced as both fundamentally wrong and also futile, inasmuch as, prediction tables notwithstanding, prognoses of recidivism are far from reliable, as Hood has scornfully but not unjustly observed.

Recently these objections have been carried to extravagant lengths by some criminologists, thus bringing into exceptionally sharp focus the unresolved conflict of views as to the *raison d'etre* of the penal system. Thus Professor Terence Morris has categorically declared that "the protection of society is *not* (italics original) the prime consideration of the criminal law. And there is no reason why it ought to be, unless we are throwing overboard the concepts of justice and desert."[6] But if criminals do not damage society, why should they "deserve" any punishment? So also in similar vein, Roger Hood has pleaded for a return to a system which bases the length of sentences "more on moral evaluation than on appeals to the utilitarian philosophy of deterrence and reductivism."[7] These proposals are, however, open to the retort that, although prediction techniques are still not as reliable as could be wished, they are at least open to objective testing, which should provide data by which their reliability may reasonably be expected to improve; whereas the validity of moral evaluations of the relative wickedness of different criminal

[6] "The Case for Abolishing Parole," *New Society*, June 19, 1980.

[7] Hood, Roger, *Tolerance and the Tariff* (National Association for the Care and Resettlement of Offenders, 1974), p. 7.

acts is merely a matter of opinion and cannot in the nature of the case ever be subjected to any objective test. Moreover the fleeting character of such appraisals is only too clearly demonstrated by the incongruity of the penalties listed on page 41 as judged by contemporary standards.

It seems, therefore, that we are in for a period in which the traditional moralistic and punitive attitude will dominate the penal process. This will of itself encourage the survival of the distinction between acts which are *mala prohibita* and those which are *mala in se*; and in relation to the latter it will raise all the difficulties (discussed in my lecture on pp. 38 *et seq.*) consequent upon the fact that a finding of guilt requires not only that the accused should have performed an unlawful act, but that he should have done so with criminal intent. In that context, I would particularly emphasise the argument on pages 46 *et seq.* that the concept of *mens rea* should not necessarily constitute an essential element in the *definition* of a crime, but that in an increasing number of cases an offender's intent is relevant only to the way in which he should be dealt with after proof of his criminal act, as already happens in "strict liability" cases where the act itself constitutes the crime, whether it was the result of deliberate intention or carelessness or negligence. (Incidentally the substitution of "reckless" for "dangerous" driving as the cause of motoring deaths was obviously intended to smuggle an element of *mens rea* into the actual definition of the crime, with the results already mentioned on p. 28.)

Finally I should like to re-emphasise the argument on page 115 that an increase in strict liability offences would be merely the latest adaptation of the long evolution of our legal system to the changing conditions of human life and to the growth of human understanding. That system is already outdated in a world in which negligence, carelessness and indifference cause more injury and damage than the total that is attributable to deliberate intent. Moreover, in virtue of its essentially punitive nature that system is bound to look to the past, not to the future, while it presumes an ability to make judgements about other men's intentions and the degree of their iniquity, the validity of which cannot ever be objectively demonstrated.

Chapter 3

THE PROBLEM OF THE MENTALLY
ABNORMAL OFFENDER

The problem of the mentally abnormal offender raises in a particularly acute form the question of the primary function of the courts. If that function is conceived as punitive, mental abnormality must be related to guilt; for a severely subnormal offender must be less blameworthy, and ought therefore to incur a less severe punishment, than one of greater intelligence who has committed an otherwise similar crime, even though he may well be a worse risk for the future. But from the preventive standpoint it is this future risk which matters, and the important question to be asked is not: does his abnormality mitigate or even obliterate his guilt? but, rather, is he a suitable subject for medical, in preference to any other, type of treatment? In short, the punitive and the preventive are respectively concerned the one with culpability and the other with treatability.

In keeping with its traditional obsession with the concept of guilt, English criminal law has, at least until lately, been chiefly concerned with the effect of mental disorder upon culpability. In recent years, however, the idea that an offender's mental state might also have a bearing on his treatability has begun to creep into the picture—with the result that the two concepts now lie somewhat uneasily side by side in what has become a very complex pattern.

Under the present law there are at least six distinct legal formulae under which an accused person's mental state may be put in issue in a criminal case. First, he may be found unfit to plead, in which case of course no trial takes place at all, unless and until he is thought to have sufficiently recovered. Second, on a charge of murder (and theoretically in other cases also) a defendant may be found to be insane within the terms of the M'Naughten Rules, by the illogical verdict of "guilty but insane" which, to be consistent with the normal use of the term guilt, ought to be revised to read—as it once did—"not guilty by reason of insanity."[1] Third, a person accused of murder can plead diminished responsibility under section 2 of the 1957 Homicide Act, in which case, if this defence succeeds, a verdict of manslaughter will be substituted for one of murder.

Up to this point it is, I think, indisputable that it is the relation between the accused's mental state and his culpability or punishability which is in issue. Obviously a man who cannot be tried cannot be punished. Again, one who is insane may have to be deprived of his liberty in the interests of the public safety, but, since an insane person is not held to be blameworthy in the same way as one who is in full possession of his faculties, the institution to which he is committed must be of a medical not a penal character; and for the same reason, he could not be hung while capital punishment was in force. So also under the Homicide Act a defence of diminished responsibility opens the door to milder punishments than the mandatory sentences of death or life imprisonment which have hitherto automatically followed verdicts of murder. Moreover, the fact that diminished responsibility is conceived in terms of reduced culpability, and not as indicative of the need for medical treatment, is further illustrated by the fact that in less than half the cases in which this defence has succeeded since the courts have had power to make hospital orders under the 1959 Mental Health Act, have such orders actually been made.[2] In the great majority of all the successful cases under section 2 of the Homicide Act a sentence of imprisonment has been imposed, the duration of this ranging from life to a matter of not more than a few months.

---

[1] Since 1964 the formula has been thus revised.
[2] House of Lords Official Report, May 1, 1963, col. 174.

Moreover, the Court of Appeal has indicated[3] approval of such sentences on the ground that a verdict of manslaughter based on diminished responsibility implies that a "residue of responsibility" rests on the accused person and that this "residue of criminal intent" surely presents a sentencing judge with a problem of nice mathematical calculation as to the appropriate measure of punishment.

Under the Mental Health Act of 1959, however, the notion of reduced culpability begins to be complicated by the alternative criterion of treatability. Section 60 of that Act provides the fourth and fifth of my six formulae. Under the first subsection of this section an offender who is convicted at a higher court (or at a magistrates' court if his offence is one which carries liability to imprisonment) may be compulsorily detained in hospital, or made subject to a guardianship order, if the court is satisfied, on the evidence of two doctors (one of whom must have special experience in the diagnosis or treatment of mental disorders) that this is in all the circumstances the most appropriate way of dealing with him. In the making of such orders emphasis is clearly on the future, not on the past: the governing consideration is not whether the offender deserves to be punished, but whether in fact medical treatment is likely to succeed. No sooner have we said this, however, than the old concept of culpability rears its head again. For a hospital order made by a higher court may be accompanied by a restriction order of either specified or indefinite duration, during the currency of which the patient may only be discharged on the order of the Home Secretary; and a magistrates' court also, although it has no similar power itself to make a restriction order, may commit an offender to the Crown Court to be dealt with, if it is of the opinion that, having regard to the nature of the offence, the antecedents of the offender and the risk of his committing further offences if set at liberty,

[3] *R.* v. *James* [1961] Crim.L.R. 842.

a hospital order should be accompanied by a restriction order.

The restriction order is thus professedly designed as a protection to the public; but a punitive element also, I think, still lingers in it. For if the sole object was the protection of the public against the premature discharge of a mentally disordered dangerous offender, it could hardly be argued that the court's prediction of the safe moment for release, perhaps years ahead, is likely to be more reliable than the judgment at the appropriate time of the hospital authorities who will have had the patient continuously under their surveillance.[4] If their purpose is purely protective, all orders ought surely to be of indefinite duration, and the fact that this is not so suggests that they are still tainted with the tariff notion of sentencing—that is to say, with the idea that a given offence "rates" a certain period of loss of liberty. Certainly, on any other interpretation the judges who have imposed restriction orders on offenders to run for ten or more years must credit themselves with truly remarkable powers of medical prognosis. In fairness, however, it should be said that the practice of imposing indefinite rather than fixed term orders now seems to be growing.

So, too, with the fifth of my formulae, which is to be found in subsection (2) of section 60 of the same Act. Under this, an offender who is charged before a magistrates' court with an offence for which he could be imprisoned, may be made the subject of a hospital or guardianship order *without being convicted*, provided that the court is satisfied that he did the act or made the omission of which

---

[4] One curious feature of this provision is the fact that a hospital order can apparently be made on a diagnosis of mental disorder, even if the disorder has no connection with the offence. See the Court of Criminal Appeal's judgment in the unsuccessful appeal of *R.* v. *Hatt* ([1962] Crim.L.R. 647) in which the appellant claimed that his predilection for unnecessary surgical operations had no connection with his no less fervent passion for making off with other people's cars.

he is accused. This power, however (which is itself an extended version of section 24 of the Criminal Justice Act, 1948, and has indeed a longer statutory history), may only be exercised if the accused is diagnosed as suffering from either mental illness or severe subnormality. It is not available in the case of persons suffering from either of the two other forms of mental disorder recognised by the 1959 Act, namely psychopathy, or simple, as distinct from severe, subnormality. And why not? One can only presume that the reason for this restriction is the fear that in cases in which only moderate mental disorder is diagnosed, or in which the diagnosis is particularly difficult and a mistake might easily be made, an offender might escape the punishment that he deserved. Even though no hospital or guardianship order can be made unless the court is of opinion that this is the "most suitable" method of disposing of the case, safeguards against the risk that this method might be used for the offender who really deserved to be punished are still written into the law.

One curious ambiguity in subsection 6 (2), however, deserves notice at this stage. Before a hospital order is made the court must be satisfied that the accused "did the act, or made the omission with which he is charged." Yet what, one may ask, is the meaning, in this context, of "the act"? Except in the case of crimes of absolute liability, a criminal charge does not relate to a purely physical action. It relates to a physical action accompanied by a guilty mind or malicious intention. If then a person is so mentally disordered as to be incapable of forming such an intention, is he not strictly incapable of performing the act with which he is charged? Such an interpretation would, of course, make nonsense of the section, and one must presume, therefore, that the words "the act" must be construed to refer solely to the prohibited physical action, irrespective of the actor's state of mind. But in that case the effect of this subsection would seem to be to transfer every type of crime, in the case of persons of severely disordered mentality, to the category of offences of absolute liability. In practice little use appears to be made of this provision (and in my experience few magistrates are aware of its existence); but there would seem to be an important principle here, potentially capable, as I hope to suggest later, of wider application.

The last of my six formulae, which, however, ante-dates all the others, stands in a category by itself. It is to be found in section 4 of the Criminal Justice Act of 1948, under which a court may make mental treatment (residential or non-residential) a condition of a probation order, provided that the offender's mental condition is "such as requires and as may be susceptible to treatment," but is not such as to justify his being in the language of that day certified as "of unsound mind" or "mentally defective." Such a provision represents a very whole-hearted step in the direction of accepting the criterion of treatability. For, although those to whom this section may be applied must be deemed to be guilty—in the sense that they have been convicted of offences involving *mens rea*—the only question to be decided is that of their likely response to medical or other treatment. Moreover, apart from the exclusion of insanity or mental defect, no restriction is placed on the range of diagnostic categories who may be required to submit to mental treatment under this section, although as always in the case of a probation order imposed on adults, the order cannot be made without the probationer's own consent. Nor is any reference anywhere made or even implied as to the effect of their mental condition upon their culpability. It is of interest, too, that, in practice, the use of these provisions has not been confined to what are often regarded as "pathological" crimes. Dr. Grunhut who made a study of cases to which the section was applied in 1953[5] found that out of a total of 636 probationers, 275 had committed offences against property, 216 sexual offences, 97 offences of violence

[5] Grunhut, M., *Probation and Mental Treatment* (Tavistock Publications, 1963).

(other than sexual) and 48 other types of offence. Some of the property crimes had, it is true, "an apparently pathological background," but no less than 48 per cent. were classified as "normal" acquisitive thefts.

All these modifications in the criminal process in the case of the mentally abnormal offender thus tend (with the possible exception of the 1948 Act) to treat such abnormality as in greater or less degree exculpatory. Their purpose is not just to secure that medical treatment should be provided for any offender likely to benefit from this, but rather to guard against the risk that the mentally disordered will be unjustly punished. Their concern with treatability, where it occurs, is in effect consequential rather than primary. The question whether the doctors can help him thus follows upon a negative answer to the prior question: is he really to blame?

Nowhere is this more conspicuous than in section 2 of the Homicide Act; and it was indeed from a study of the operation of that section that I was led nearly four years ago to the conclusion that this was the wrong approach; that any attempt to distinguish between wickedness and mental abnormality was doomed to failure; and that the only solution for the future was to allow the concept of responsibility to "wither away" and to concentrate instead on the problem of the choice of treatment, without attempting to assess the effect of mental peculiarities or degrees of culpability. That opinion was based on a study of the files of some seventy-three cases in which a defence of diminished responsibility had been raised,[6] which were kindly made available by the Home Office. To these have since been added the records of another 126 cases, the two series together covering the five and a half years from the time that the Act came into force down to mid-September 1962.

Before I pursue the implications of the suggestion that

[6] Wootton, Barbara, "Diminished Responsibility: A Layman's View" (1960) 76 *Law Quarterly Review* 224.

the concept of responsibility should be allowed to wither away, it may be well to ask whether anything in later material calls for any modification of my earlier conclusion. I do not think it does. Indeed the experience of the past three and a half years seems to have high-lighted both the practical and the philosophical difficulty—or as I would prefer to say the impossibility—of assessing other people's responsibility for their actions.

Some new issues have, however, arisen in the struggle to interpret the relevant section of the Act. Much legal argument has, for example, been devoted to the effect of drink upon responsibility. The Act provides that a charge of murder may result in a conviction for manslaughter if the accused was suffering from "such abnormality of mind (whether arising from a condition of arrested or retarded development of mind or any inherent causes or induced by disease or injury) as substantially impaired his responsibility for his acts." Accordingly, it has been suggested that the transient effect of drink, if sufficient to produce a toxic effect upon the brain, might amount to an "injury" within the meaning of the Act. Alternatively (in the picturesque phrase of one defence counsel) drink might "make up the deficit" necessary to convert a pre-existent minor abnormality into a substantial impairment of responsibility. None of these issues has yet been authoritatively decided. Sometimes the court has been able to wriggle out of a decision, as the Court of Appeal did when the "injury" argument was used on behalf of Di Duca,[7] on the ground that the particular offender concerned, whether drunk or sober, showed insufficient evidence of abnormality. Sometimes the opposite escape route has been available, as when the trial judge in the case of *Dowdall,*[8] while careful to emphasise that the section was not to be regarded as "a drunkard's charter," reminded the jury that two doctors had testified to the defendant's gross abnormality even apart from his

[7] *R.* v. *Di Duca* [1959] 43 Cr.App.R. 167.

admitted addiction to liquor. In *Samuel's*[8] case, on the other hand, in which the "deficit" theory was strongly argued in the absence of the jury, the judge clearly regarded it as inadmissible and made no reference to it in his summing up. But nearly two years later the Court of Appeal[9] concluded its judgment in *Clarke's* appeal with a statement that

> "the court wished to make it clear that it had not considered the effect of drink on a mind suffering from diminished responsibility. The court had not considered whether any abnormality of mind, however slight, would constitute a defence when substantially impaired by drink. That matter would have to be considered on another occasion."

After drink, insanity. A second complication has arisen in the problem of distinguishing between persons whose responsibility is merely diminished, and those who are deemed to be insane within the meaning of the M'Naughten Rules. Here there appears to be a division of opinion among the judges as to the right of the Crown to seek to establish insanity in cases in which the defence pleads only diminished responsibility. In two of my earlier series of 73 cases in which this defence was raised, and in four of the later series of 126 cases, a verdict of guilty but insane was actually returned; and in at least half a dozen others in which this defence did succeed, the witnesses called by the Crown to rebut evidence of diminished responsibility sought to establish that the accused was in fact insane. Such a procedure was in keeping with the forecast of the Attorney-General in his speech on the Second Reading of the Homicide Bill.[10] "If," he said,

> "the defence raise any question as to the accused's mental capacity, and evidence is called to show that

---

[8] Unpublished transcript.

[9] *R.* v. *Clarke* [1962] Crim.L.R. 836.

[10] House of Commons Official Report, Vol. 560 (November 15, 1956), col. 1252.

> he is suffering from a serious abnormality of mind, then, if the evidence goes beyond a diminution of responsibility and really shows that the accused was within the M'Naughten Rules, it would be right for the judge to leave it to the jury to determine whether the accused was, to use the old phrase, 'guilty but insane,' or to return a verdict of manslaughter on the basis that, although not insane, he suffered from diminished responsibility . . . "

Nevertheless in the case of *Price* in 1962[11] the trial judge ruled that

> "if the Crown raises the issue of insanity and the jury find the accused guilty but insane, he cannot challenge the verdict in any higher court . . . It seems to me, having regard to the serious consequences which would follow to a man if the Crown does succeed in raising the issue of insanity that the law cannot be, without an Act of Parliament, that a man should lose his right of appeal. In these circumstances I rule that the Crown is not entitled to invite the jury to consider the issue of insanity."

If this ruling is upheld, the result will be that the—at the best of times exceptionally difficult—distinction between insanity and diminished responsibility will be unlikely to be drawn on the merits of the case. For, except in extreme cases, the defence is always likely to prefer a plea of diminished responsibility to one of insanity, since if the latter succeeds indefinite detention necessarily follows, whereas on a conviction for manslaughter, which is the outcome of a successful defence of diminished responsibility, the court has complete discretion to pass whatever sentence it thinks fit. Persons who may be insane within the meaning of the M'Naughten Rules are therefore always likely to be tempted to plead diminished responsibility. Yet if they do, the jury will, if the analogy of the judgment in *Price's* case is followed, be precluded

---

[11] *R.* v. *Price* [1962] 3 All E.R. 960.

from hearing evidence as to their possible insanity and so arriving at an informed judgment on the issue of diminished responsibility versus insanity.

These developments can only be said to have added to the prevailing confusion. One other step has, however, been taken, which does at least aim at clarification. In the early days of the Act's operation juries were generally given little guidance as to the meaning of diminished responsibility. Judges did not ordinarily go beyond making sure that the members of the jury were familiar with the actual words of the section, which they were then expected to interpret for themselves. In 1960, however, in allowing the appeal of Patrick Byrne, the Birmingham Y.W.C.A. murderer, the Court of Appeal[1][2] attempted a formulation of the meaning of diminished responsibility on which judges have subsequently been able to draw in their directions to juries. In the words used by the Lord Chief Justice in this judgment "abnormality of mind" must be defined widely enough "to cover the mind's activities in all its aspects, not only the perception of physical acts and matters, and the ability to form a rational judgment as to whether an act is right or wrong, but also the ability to exercise willpower to control physical acts in accordance with that rational judgment." Furthermore, while medical evidence on this issue was said to be "no doubt of importance," it was not necessarily conclusive and might be outweighed by other material. Juries might also legitimately differ from doctors in assessing whether any impairment of responsibility could properly be regarded as "substantial"; and to guide them on this last point it was suggested that such phrases as "partial insanity" or on "the borderline of insanity" might be possible interpretations of the kind of abnormality which would substantially impair responsibility.

How far this helps may be a matter for argument. Subsequently, in the case of Victor Terry, the Worthing bank

---

[1][2] *R.* v. *Byrne* (1960) 44 Cr.App.R. 246.

murderer, Mr. Justice Stable adopted the original course of handing the jury a transcript of the (exceptionally voluminous) medical evidence instead of attempting to sum this up himself; but this procedure did not commend itself to the Court of Appeal,[13] although the court's disapproval did not go so far as to result in the condemned man's appeal being allowed or save him from being hanged. Certainly for my part I cannot think that anyone can listen to, or read, the sophisticated subtleties in which legal disputations about degrees of responsibility persistently flounder and founder, without reaching the paradoxical conclusion that the harder we try to recognise the complexity of reality, the greater the unreality of the whole discussion. Indeed it is hardly surprising that in practice most of these subtleties probably pass over the heads of juries, whose conclusions appear to be reached on simpler grounds. At least two-thirds of those persons in whose cases a defence of diminished responsibility has succeeded have produced some serious evidence of previous mental instability such as a history of previous attempts at suicide, or of discharge from the Forces on psychiatric grounds, or of some trouble for which psychiatric advice has been sought, while a much higher proportion, though not medically diagnosed, are thought by relatives to be in some way peculiar. On the other hand, well under half of those in whose case a defence of diminished responsibility was not successful appear to have had any history of mental instability. It would seem that juries, clutching perhaps at straws, are disposed to take the view that a previous history of mental disturbance indicates (on the balance of probability, which is all that they have to establish) subsequent impairment of responsibility. And in the remaining cases, in which there is no such history, the concept of diminished responsibility seems to be dissolving into what is virtually the equivalent of a mitigating circumstance. Certainly in many of the

[13] *R.* v. *Terry* (1961) 45 Cr.App.R. 180.

more recent cases it is difficult to establish the presence of mental abnormality unless by the circular argument that anybody who commits homicide must, by definition, be unbalanced. It was surely compassion rather than evidence of mental abnormality which accounted for the success of a defence of diminished responsibility in the case of the major who found himself the father of a Mongol baby and, after reading up the subject of Mongolism in his public library, decided that the best course for everybody concerned would be to smother the child. And in the not infrequent cases in which a defence of diminished responsibility has succeeded, when homicide has resulted from such common human motives as sexual jealousy or the desire to escape from pecuniary embarrassment, it is hard not to believe that juries were moved more by the familiarity, than by the abnormality, of the offender's mental processes.

The most important development of the past few years lies, however, in the fact that the impossibility of keeping a clear line between the wicked and the weak-minded seems now to be officially admitted. In the judgment of the Court of Appeal on Byrne's appeal, from which I have already quoted, the Lord Chief Justice frankly admitted that "the step between "he did not resist his impulse,' and 'he could not resist his impulse' " was one which was "incapable of scientific proof. *A fortiori*," the judgment continues, "there is no scientific measurement of the degree of difficulty which an abnormal person finds in controlling his impulses. These problems which in the present state of medical knowledge are scientifically insoluble the jury can only approach in a broad common-sense way."

Apart from admiration of the optimism which expects common sense to make good the deficiencies of science, it is only necessary to add that the problem would seem to be insoluble, not merely in the present, but indeed in any, state of medical knowledge. Improved medical knowledge may certainly be expected to give better insight into the origins of mental abnormalities, and better predictions as to the probability that particular types of individuals will in fact "control their physical acts" or make "rational judgments"; but neither medical nor any other science can ever hope to prove whether a man who does not resist his impulses does not do so because he cannot or because he will not. The propositions of science are by definition subject to empirical validation; but since it is not possible to get inside another man's skin, no objective criterion which can distinguish between "he did not" and "he could not" is conceivable.

Logic, experience and the Lord Chief Justice thus all appear to lead to the same conclusion—that is to say, to the impossibility of establishing any reliable measure of responsibility in the sense of a man's ability to have acted otherwise than as he did. After all, every one of us can say with St. Paul (who, as far as I am aware, is not generally suspected of diminished responsibility) "the good that I would I do not: but the evil which I would not, that I do."

I have dealt at some length with our experience of diminished responsibility cases under the Homicide Act on account of three facts, first, that under this Act questions of responsibility have to be decided before and not after conviction; second, that these questions fall to be decided by juries; and, third, that the charges involved are of the utmost gravity. These three facts together have caused the relationship of responsibility to culpability to be explored with exceptional thoroughness in this particular context. But the principles involved are by no means restricted to the narrow field of charges of homicide. They have a far wider applicability, and are indeed implicit also in section 60 of the Mental Health Act. It seems inevitable that if in any case a convicted person wished (as might well happen) to challenge the diagnosis of mental disorder which must precede the making of a hospital order, he would quickly be plunged into arguments about subnormality and psychopathy closely parallel to those which occupy so many hours of diminished responsibility trials.

At the same time the proposal that we should bypass, or disregard, the concept of responsibility is only too easily misunderstood; and I propose, therefore, to devote the remainder of this lecture to an attempt to meet some of the criticisms which have been brought against this proposal: to clarify just what it does or does not mean in the present context and to examine its likely implications.

First, it is to be observed that the term "responsibility" is here used in a restricted sense, much narrower than that which it often carries in ordinary speech. The measure of a person's responsibility for his actions is perhaps best defined in the words that I used earlier in terms of his capacity to act otherwise than as he did. A person may be described as totally irresponsible if he is wholly incapable of controlling his actions, and as being in a state of diminished responsibility if it is abnormally difficult for him to control them. Responsibility in this restricted sense is not to be confused with the sense in which a man is often said to be responsible for an action if he has in fact committed it. The questions: who broke the window? and could the man who broke the window have prevented himself from doing so? are obviously quite distinct. To dismiss the second as unanswerable in no way diminishes the importance of finding an answer to the first. Hence the primary job of the courts in determining by whom a forbidden act has actually been committed is wholly unaffected by any proposal to disregard the question of responsibility in the narrower sense. Indeed the only problem that arises here is linguistic, inasmuch as one is accustomed to say that X was "responsible" for breaking the window when the intention is to convey no more than that he did actually break it. Another word is needed here (and I must confess that I have not succeeded in finding one) to describe "responsibility" for doing an action as distinct from inability to refrain from doing it. "Accountable" has sometimes been suggested, but its usage in this sense is often awkward. "Instrumental" is perhaps better, though one could still wish for an adjective such perhaps as "agential" derived from the word "agent." However, all that matters is to keep firmly in mind that responsibility in the present context has nothing to do with the authorship of an act, only with the state of mind of its author.

In the second place, to discard the notion of responsibility does not mean that the mental condition of an offender ceases to have any importance, or that psychiatric considerations become irrelevant. The difference is that they become relevant, not to the question of determining the measure of his culpability, but to the choice of the treatment most likely to be effective in discouraging him from offending again; and even if these two aspects of the matter may be related, this is not to be dismissed as a distinction without a difference. The psychiatrist to whom it falls to advise as to the probable response of an offender to medical treatment no doubt has his own opinion as to the man's capacity for self-control; and doubtless also those opinions are a factor in his judgment as to the outlook for medical treatment, or as to the probability that the offence will be repeated. But these are, and must remain, matters of opinion, "incapable," in Lord Parker's words, "of scientific proof." Opinions as to treatability, on the other hand, as well as predications as to the likelihood of further offences can be put to the test of experience and so proved right or wrong. And by systematic observation of that experience, it is reasonable to expect that a body of knowledge will in time be built up, upon which it will be possible to draw, in the attempt to choose the most promising treatment in future cases.

Next, it must be emphasised that nothing in what has been said involves acceptance of a deterministic view of human behaviour. It is an indisputable fact of experience that human beings do respond predictably to various stimuli—whether because they choose to or because they can do no other it is not necessary to inquire. There are cases in which medical treatment works: there are cases in which it fails. Equally there are cases in which deterrent penalties appear to deter those upon whom they are imposed from committing further offences; and there are cases in which they do not. Once the criminal law is conceived as an instrument of crime prevention, it is these facts which demand attention, and from which we can learn to improve the efficiency of that instrument; and the question whether on any occasion a man could or could not have acted otherwise than as he did can be left on one side or answered either way, as may be preferred. It is no longer relevant, unless as evidence of his probable future power of self-control.

Failure to appreciate this has, I think, led to conflicts between psychiatry and the law being often fought on the wrong ground. Even so radical a criminologist as Dr. Sheldon Glueck seems to see the issue as one between

> "those who stress the prime social need of blameworthiness and retributive punishment as the coreconcept in crime and justice and those who, under the impact of psychiatric, psycho-analytic, sociological, and anthropological views insist that man's choices are the product of forces largely beyond his conscious control. . . ."[14]

Indeed Dr. Glueck's discussion of the relation of psychiatry to law is chiefly devoted to an analysis of the exculpatory effect of psychiatric knowledge, and to the changes that have been, or should be, made in the assessment of guilt as the result of the growth of this knowledge. In consequence much intellectual ingenuity is wasted in refining the criteria by which the wicked may be distinguished from the weak-minded. For surely to argue thus is to argue from the wrong premises: the real difference between the psychiatric and the legal approach has nothing to do with free will and determinism. It has to do with rival conceptions of the objectives of the criminal process, with the question whether the aim of that process is punitive or pre-

[14] Glueck, Sheldon, *Law and Psychiatry* (Tavistock Publications, 1962), p. 6.

ventive, whether what matters is to punish the wrongdoer or to set him on the road to virtue; and, in order to take a stand on that issue, neither party need be a determinist.

So much for what disregard of responsibility does not mean. What, in a more positive sense, is it likely to involve? Here, I think, one of the most important consequences must be to obscure the present rigid distinction between the penal and the medical institution. As things are, the supposedly fully responsible are consigned to the former: only the wholly or partially irresponsible are eligible for the latter. Once it is admitted that we have no reliable criterion by which to distinguish between those two categories, strict segregation of each into a distinct set of institutions becomes absurd and impracticable. For purposes of convenience offenders for whom medical treatment is indicated will doubtless tend to be allocated to one building, and those for whom medicine has nothing to offer to another; but the formal distinction between prison and hospital will become blurred, and, one may reasonably expect, eventually obliterated altogether. Both will be simply "places of safety" in which offenders receive the treatment which experience suggests is most likely to evoke the desired response.

Does this mean that the distinction between doctors and prison officers must also become blurred? Up to a point it clearly does. At the very least it would seem that some fundamental implications for the medical profession must be involved when the doctor becomes part of the machinery of law enforcement. Not only is the normal doctor-patient relationship profoundly disturbed, but far-reaching questions also arise as to the nature of the condition which the doctor is called upon to treat. If a tendency to break the law is not in itself to be classified as a disease, which does he seek to cure—the criminality or the illness? To the medical profession these questions, which I have discussed at length elsewhere,[15] must be of primary concern. But

[15] Wootton, Barbara, "The Law, The Doctor and The Deviant," *British Medical Journal*, July 27, 1963.

for present purposes it may be more relevant to notice how, as so often happens in this country, changes not yet officially recognised in theory are quietly creeping in by the back door. Already the long-awaited institution at Grendon Underwood is administered as an integral part of the prison system; yet the regime is frankly medical. Its purpose has been described by the Prison Commission's Director of Medical Services as the investigation and treatment of mental disorder generally recognised as calling for a psychiatric approach; the investigation of the mental condition of offenders whose offences in themselves suggest mental instability; and an exploration of the problem of the treatment of the psychopath. Recommendations for admission must come from prison medical officers, and the prison itself is under the charge of a medical superintendent with wide experience in psychiatry.[16]

Grendon Underwood (unless one should include Broadmoor and one or two others which have a much narrower scope) is the first genuinely hybrid institution. Interchange between medical and penal institutions is, however, further facilitated by the power of the Home Secretary under section 72 of the Mental Health Act to transfer to hospital persons whom, on appropriate medical evidence, he finds to be suffering from mental disorder of a nature or degree to warrant their detention in a hospital for medical treatment. Such transfers have the same effect as does a hospital order, and they may be (and usually are) also accompanied by an order restricting discharge. It is, moreover, of some interest that transfers are sometimes made quite soon after the court has passed sentence. Out of six cases convicted under section 2 of the Homicide Act in which transfers under section 72 were effected, three were removed to hospital

---

[16] Snell, H. K. (Director of Medical Services, Prison Commission), "H.M. Prison Grendon," *British Medical Journal*, September 22, 1962.

less than three months after sentence.[17] Although it is, of course, always possible that the prisoner had been mentally normal at the time of his offence and had only suffered a mental breakdown later, transfer after a relatively short period does indicate at least a possibility that in the judgment of the Home Secretary some mental abnormality may have been already present either at the time of sentence or even when the crime was committed.[18]

The courts, however, seem to be somewhat jealous of the exercise of this power, which virtually allows the Home Secretary to treat as sick, persons whom they have sentenced to imprisonment and presumably regard as wicked. Indeed it seems that, if a diagnosis of mental disorder is to be made, the courts hold that it is, generally speaking, their business, and not the Home Secretary's, to make it. So at least it would appear from the judgments of the Court of Appeal in the cases of Constance Ann James[19] and Philip Morris,[20] both of whom had been found guilty of manslaughter on grounds of diminished responsibility and had been sentenced to imprisonment. In the former case, in which the evidence as to the accused's mental condition was unchallenged, the trial judge apparently had misgivings about the public safety and in particular the safety of the convicted woman's younger child whose brother she had killed. He therefore passed a sentence of three years' imprisonment, leaving it, as he said, to the appropriate authorities to make further inquiries so that the Secretary of State might, if he thought fit, transfer the prisoner to hospital under section 72 of the Mental Health Act. The appeal was allowed, on the ground that there was obviously no need for punishment and that there were reasonable hopes that the disorder from which

---

[17] See also Postscript to this chapter, p. 93.

[18] See Postscript to this chapter, p. 93, for later figures about such transfers.

[19] *R.* v. *James* [1961] Crim.L.R. 842.

[20] *R.* v. *Morris* (1961) 45 Cr.App.R. 233.

the woman suffered would prove curable. In the circumstances, though reluctant to interfere with the discretion of the sentencing court, the Court of Appeal substituted a hospital order accompanied by an indefinite restriction.

In Philip Morris' case, in which, however, the appellant was unsuccessful, the matter was put even more clearly. Again the trial judge had refused to make a hospital order on grounds of the public safety and, failing any vacancy in a secure hospital, had passed a sentence of life imprisonment. But on this the Court of Appeal commented as follows:

> "Although the discretion . . . is very wide indeed, the basic principle must be that in the ordinary case where punishment as such is not intended, and where the sole object of the sentence is that a man should receive mental treatment, and be at large as soon as he can safely be discharged, a proper exercise of the discretion demands that steps should be taken to exercise the powers under section 60 and that the matter should not be left to be dealt with by the Secretary of State under section 72."

These difficulties are, one may hope, of a transitional nature. They would certainly not arise if all sentences involving loss of liberty were indeterminate in respect of the type of institution in which the offender is to be detained: still less if rigid distinctions between medical and penal institutions were no longer maintained. The elimination of those distinctions, moreover, though unthinkable in a primarily punitive system which must at all times segregate the blameworthy from the blameless, is wholly in keeping with a criminal law which is preventive rather than punitive in intention.

In this lecture and in that which preceded it I have tried to signpost the road towards such a conception of the law, and to indicate certain landmarks which suggest that this is the road along which we are, if hesitantly, already treading. At first blush it might seem that strict liability and mental abnormality have not much in common; but both present a challenge to traditional views as to the point at which, and the purpose for which, considerations of guilty intent become relevant; and both illustrate the contemporary tendency to use the criminal law to protect the community against damage, no matter what might be the state of mind of those by whom that damage is done. In this context, perhaps, the little-noticed provisions of section 60 (2) of the Mental Health Act, with its distinction between the forbidden act and the conviction, along with the liberal implications of section 4 of the 1948 Criminal Justice Act, with its emphasis on treatability rather than culpability, are to be seen as the writing on the wall. And perhaps, too, it is significant that Dr. Glueck, notwithstanding his immediate preoccupation with definitions of responsibility, lets fall, almost as if with a sigh, the forecast that some day it may be possible "to limit criminal law to matters of behavior alone," and that in his concluding lecture he foresees the "twilight of futile blameworthiness."[21] That day may be still a long way off: but at least it seems to be nearer than it was.

[21] Glueck, Sheldon, *Law and Psychiatry* (Tavistock Publications, 1962), pp. 33, 147.

Every penal system which purports to punish offenders in accordance with their deserts operates on the presumption that crimes are committed deliberately by people who intend the natural consequences of their actions, and assesses the degree of their culpability on this basis. Sooner or later, however, cases are bound to turn up in which, owing to some mental abnormality, this presumption appears not to be justified. In this country, as recorded in the text of my lecture, since the middle of the last century, persons charged with murder who were found to be insane within the McNaughten definition escaped the mandatory sentence for their crime - but only at the price of being confined in what was formerly known as a "criminal lunatic asylum" during Her Majesty's pleasure. Next, the 1957 Homicide Act introduced the concept of diminished responsibility, allowing a charge of murder to be reduced to manslaughter if the accused successfully pleaded that he suffered from this condition.

The McNaughten Rules did at least define insanity objectively, but the Homicide Act's definition of diminished responsibility is virtually tautological. The statutory formula quoted on page 72 amounts to no more than a statement that an offender suffers from diminished responsibility if anything has impaired his responsibility.

Neither the McNaughten Rules nor the Homicide Act implied any change in the objective of the penal system: they were merely attempts to adjust to contemporary conceptions of mental abnormality the principle that the punishment should fit the criminal as well as the crime. One interesting result has, however, been the virtual disappearance of pleas of insanity. Thus in 1954 out of 60 cases for trial on murder charges, eight were found insane on arraignment and a further 22 guilty but insane; in 1955

out of 79 cases for trial, 13 were found insane on arraignment and 24 guilty but insane; and in 1956 again out of 79
cases, 14 were found insane on arraignment and 18 guilty
but insane. When, however, it comes to more recent times,
the picture is quite different. In 1976, out of 149 cases the
number found "unfit to plead" fell to three and only two
were found not guilty by reason of insanity (as the verdict
now reads); and out of 162 cases in 1977, the figures
were one unfit to plead, and one not guilty by reason of
insanity; while for 1978 out of 130 cases, one was found
unfit to plead and none not guilty on ground of insanity.
Meanwhile, convictions for manslaughter with diminished
responsibility have leapt up from 25 in 1958 to 79 in
1978, and have in fact virtually become hardly more than
an escape route from the mandatory sentence for murder.

The 1959 Mental Health Act, however, went much
further. Section 4 of the Act listed four types of mental
disorder (mental illness, severe subnormality, subnormality
and psychopathic disorder), the last three (but not mental
illness) being more specifically defined; and the Act
established the system, referred to in my lecture, under
which an offender diagnosed as suffering from any one of
these conditions may be detained in a hospital, or placed
under the guardianship of a local authority or an approved
person. By implication it thus established the division
between the normal and the abnormal offender, with the
implication that the former were responsible for their mis-
deeds, and might properly be punished for them, while
those in the latter category were sick and in need of
medical care.

From one point of view this is fine. It means that in
cases deemed to suffer from mental disorder, treatability,
not culpability, becomes the criterion by which sentence
should be selected; and that in cases of diminished
responsibility under the 1957 Act, sentence should be
modified to take account of this abnormality. In this way
the original presumption that we are all responsible for our
wrongdoing and should be punished accordingly is under-

mined. But there are snags. To take the diminished responsibility group first, in 1978 of the 79 persons sentenced under the relevant section of the Homicide Act (*i.e.* sec. 2) 39 were nevertheless sentenced to immediate, and two to suspended, imprisonment, thus, as indicated in my lecture, imposing on the judge who passed sentence the delicate task of assessing the "residue" of responsibility.

The treatment of all cases diagnosed as suffering from any of the disorders listed in the Mental Health Act involves, however, further confusion. Logically and morally, it might be supposed that, being sick people, these cases ought all to be consigned to medical care, and to be wholly exempt from punishment. Nevertheless, section 6 (*b*) of the 1959 Act, which forbids a court to impose a fine or a probation order or to pass a sentence of imprisonment for his offence on anyone subject to a hospital or guardianship order, does not prevent the court from imprisoning a person diagnosed as suffering from one of the mental disorders recognised by the Act as *an alternative* to imposing a hospital or guardianship order. Indeed, in practice it is not uncommon for persons diagnosed as psychopaths to be committed to prison. This is generally excused as a regrettable necessity in cases which either no hospital is willing to accept, or in which a hospital that will accept is thought to be insufficiently secure. But when Professor Trevor Gibbens followed up for eight years a group of "particularly severe" cases of offenders diagnosed as psychopaths who had nevertheless been imprisoned and matched these against a supposedly normal group of prisoners with similar criminal histories, he concluded that "whatever the prognosis of the psychopath may be in terms of his mental state, his criminal prognosis appears to be . . . not very different from that of any other man with the same number of previous convictions."[1]

[1] Quoted in Walker, Professor Nigel, and McCabe, Sarah, *Crime and Insanity in England*, Vol. 2, p. 232 (Edinburgh University Press, 1973).

The upshot seems to be that the simple dichotomy of the law that an offender either is, or is not, responsible for his offences has produced grave moral and legal anomalies, especially in regard to persons categorised by the Mental Health Act as suffering from "psychopathic disorder" - which is statutorily defined as "a persistent disorder or disability of mind (whether or not including subnormality of intelligence) which results in abnormally aggressive or seriously irresponsible conduct on the part of the patient, and requires or is susceptible to medical treatment." This definition has, not surprisingly, been much criticised (amongst others by the late Sir Aubrey Lewis) as being circular, inasmuch as the psychopath's mental disorder is inferred from his anti-social behaviour, while the anti-social behaviour is itself explained by his mental disorder. Lewis, on the other hand, firmly maintained that "if non-conformity can be detected only in total behaviour, while all the particular psychological functions seem unimpaired, health will be presumed, not illness."[2]

At a more fundamental level, acceptance of mental disorder as diminishing or eliminating criminal responsibility demands an ability to get inside someone else's mind so completely as to be certain whether he has acted wilfully or knowingly, and also to experience the strength of the temptations to which he is exposed. This, I submit, is beyond the competence of even the most highly qualified expert. Psychiatrists may uncover factors in patients' backgrounds (often in terms of childhood experience) by which they profess to "explain" why one individual has an urge to strangle young girls and another to rape elderly women; but these "explanations" are merely predictive of the *likelihood* of such behaviour occurring. Accessible data for scientific proof whether the temptations could have been resisted just do not exist. Nor is there any better foundation for the layman's tendency to imagine that

[2] Lewis, Sir Aubrey, *The State of Psychiatry*, pp. 179-194 (Routledge and Kegan Paul, 1967).

eccentric temptations which he has never himself experienced (such as the temptation to steal bicycles and only bicycles, or to cut off girls' hair) are harder to resist than temptations to fiddle one's expense account or to draw supplementary benefit to which one is not entitled.

I submit therefore that the present law, under which offenders must be classified as *either* mentally disordered *or* criminally responsible for their actions, not only produces anomalies but also attempts the impossible, particularly in view of the wide compass of the Mental Health Act's definition of psychopathic disorder. It is in fact difficult to think of any form of persistently objectionable behaviour which that formula could not be stretched to cover. In the end it would seem that for practical purposes we are brought to the paradoxical conclusion that, if a person's crimes are by ordinary standards only moderately objectionable, he should be regarded as wicked and liable to appropriate punishment, but if his wickedness goes beyond a certain point, it ceases to be "wickedness" at all and becomes a medical condition.

Such rigid classifications are unnatural. Nature knows only infinite gradations in both the physical and the mental differences between members of the human species, and it is even probable that not only does one individual's responsibility for his actions differ from that of another, but that the sense of responsibility in the same individual may also vary from time to time. Many women would, for example, admit that menstruation is often accompanied by a tendency to uncharacteristically irresponsible behaviour.

In view, therefore, of this widespread confusion of thought as to where wickedness ends and psychopathic disorder begins, the Government in 1972 appointed the (Butler) Committee on Mentally Abnormal Offenders with the following terms of reference:

> (a) "to consider to what extent and on what criteria the law should recognise mental disorder or abnormality in a person accused of a criminal offence

as a factor affecting his liability to be tried or convicted, and his disposal," and

(b) "to consider what, if any, changes are necessary
in the powers, procedure and facilities relating to the
provision of appropriate treatment, in prison, hospital
or the community, for offenders suffering from
mental disorder or abnormality, and to their discharge
and aftercare; and to make recommendations."

That landed the problem of distinguishing the sick,
irresponsible sheep from the wicked, responsible goats
fairly and squarely in the lap of the Committee. Although
their eventual Report shows signs of hankering after
proposals to abolish psychopathy as a legal category
altogether, they could make no such recommendation,
inasmuch as, if psychopaths are not mentally abnormal,
that would exclude them from consideration by a
Committee appointed to deal with the problems of
Mentally Abnormal Offenders.

In the end the Committee resolved their dilemma by
recommending as an addition to section 60 (i) of the 1959
Mental Health Act (which allows the court to make
hospital orders in the case of mentally disordered offenders)
a provision that

"no order shall be made under this section in the case
of an offender suffering from psychopathic disorder
with dangerous anti-social tendencies unless the court
is satisfied:

(a) that a previous mental or organic illness, or an
identifiable psychological or physical defect relevant
to the disorder, is known or suspected; and

(b) there is an expectation of therapeutic benefit
from hospital admission."

They thus accepted the Lewis doctrine. Moreover to round
the matter off, they bravely added that "properly used the
prison environment can possibly provide the situation
within which dangerous psychopaths can most readily be
helped to develop more acceptable social attitudes."

These last words were in fact merely condoning the

current practice of the courts. Unfortunately information is not available as to how many persons diagnosed as suffering from psychopathic disorder are in fact sentenced to immediate imprisonment; but we are told that

> "since 1977 prison medical officers have made returns of the number of prisoners in their care whom they consider to be suffering from mental disorder of a nature or degree which would justify transfer to hospital under the Mental Health Act 1959. The returns for 30th June and 31st December 1978 identified 377 and 389 sentenced mentally disordered prisoners."[3]

But in suggesting that prison might be the *right place* not only for men and women in full possession of their faculties whose crimes have been wilfully committed, but also for persons believed to be handicapped by some mental abnormality, the Committee not merely echoed the century-old fantasy of Lord Butler's remotely connected kinsman, the author of *Erewhon*, but frankly ignored the legal distinction between the sick and the wicked. In so doing, however, they encouraged the hope that we may be moving towards a system in which the treatment of offenders will be concentrated more upon prospects for their future than upon evaluations of their past iniquities. This is the subject of my final lecture.

---

[3] House of Lords Official Report, December 18, 1980, col. 1277.

Chapter 4

SENTENCING POLICY IN A PREVENTIVE SYSTEM

As a method of decision-making the process by which offenders are sentenced must surely be almost without parallel. All its peculiarities are indeed well enough known, but even so it may perhaps be worth briefly listing them, so as to bring the whole picture into view.

In the first place, these decisions are always of importance—often of overwhelming importance—to the individuals concerned, and in the aggregate they are highly important also to the whole community: yet they are frequently made in a very few moments, often in magistrates' courts or the Crown Court after a brief whispered discussion between the chairman and his colleagues. Second, although in many cases the court has a very wide discretion in its choice of sentence, there are no explicit rules as to how that discretion should be exercised, nor indeed any explicit principles determining the object of the whole exercise. Third, in many cases decisions as to sentences fall to be made by amateurs—indeed it might be said that all such decisions, not only those of lay magistrates, are amateurishly made, inasmuch as the subject of penology has no place in the training of a judge or a stipendiary magistrate. Fourth, sentences may be passed by persons who have no first-hand knowledge of what they imply— who have for instance no clear idea as to just how the regime prescribed by a sentence to Borstal differs from that followed in ordinary imprisonment. Fifth, the more serious the decision, the more likely it is to be made by one man alone, rather than by a group in consultation. Sixth, whatever the objective aimed at, no machinery exists by which the success or failure of particular decisions in reaching that objective may be assessed. In consequence it is impossible for anyone who passes sentences either to test his own performance or to learn from experience, and equally impossible to test the relevance of any information provided with the object of assisting the court to arrive at its decisions.

Is it then surprising that the choice between one sentence and another often seems to have remarkably little concrete effect? Speaking in the House of Commons on the Second Reading of the Criminal Justice Bill in 1960[1] Sir George Benson described how his researches showed that the success-rate of boys who had served a sentence of imprisonment was neither better nor worse than that of those who had undergone Borstal training; and that there was also no difference in the risk of subsequent reconviction as between a group who had served an average of four months, and one with an average of 15 months, in prison. Indeed, as far back as 1937 a five-year follow-up of first offenders by the Metropolitan police showed that the chances of reconviction were identical for those who had been fined, imprisoned or discharged, but slightly worse for those put on probation; while in spite of all the changes that are supposed to have been made in the prison system in the previous 25 years the proportion of male so-called "star" prisoners who were not reconvicted in the three years following discharge rose only from 82 per cent. to 87 per cent. between 1930-31 and 1953-54. Similarly Leslie Wilkins[2] has found that a comparison of 97 male offenders placed on probation by the Crown Court with a sample of comparable cases from elsewhere who had been otherwise dealt with showed no significant differences in respect of reconvictions.

These curious and disconcerting findings would seem to be susceptible of two alternative interpretations. On the

---

[1] House of Commons Official Report, November 17, 1960, cols. 598, 599.

[2] Wilkins, Leslie T., "A Small Comparative Study of the Results of Probation," *British Journal of Delinquency* (1958), Vol. VIII, No. 3.

one hand they may mask considerable individual differences in the impact of particular sentences upon particular individuals which are lost in the general totals. On the other hand they may merely be evidence that everything that we do falls very wide of the mark. By analogy, I suppose, if draughts of cold water were prescribed as a treatment for cancer, it would probably not make much difference whether the patient drank large draughts or small ones.

In any case it would seem that the sentencing process is capable of improvement. At the least we have to recognise that, as the Streatfeild Report itself emphasised,[3] the old-fashioned view that a "tariff system" under which an offender gets what he is thought to deserve can take all the possible objectives of sentencing "in its stride" is altogether too naive. Today those multiple objectives include fixing a sentence proportionate to the offender's culpability: protecting society, and deterring potential offenders, as well as deterring or reforming the individual offender himself. Nor, according to Lord Denning, must the courts overlook the "denunciatory" function of a sentence which demands that "the punishment for grave crimes should adequately reflect the revulsion felt by the great majority of citizens for them," "the ultimate justification of any punishment" being, in his Lordship's view, "not that it is a deterrent, but that it is the emphatic denunciation by the community of a crime."[4]

That there will be conflicts between these objectives can hardly be disputed. Nor is the task of resolving those conflicts or of determining their respective priorities one in which science can help, although, as I shall suggest later, there may be sound, practical reasons for preferring some to others. On the other hand, in the pursuit of any one

---

[3] Interdepartmental Committee on the Business of the Criminal Courts, *Report* (H.M.S.O., 1961), Cmnd. 1289, paras. 257-262.

[4] Royal Commission on Capital Punishment, 1949-53, *Report*, Cmd. 8932 (H.M.S.O., 1953), para. 53.

predetermined future objective it is reasonable to hope for guidance from systematic observation of past experience. Science can undoubtedly examine the effects of sentences with a view to improving their future effectiveness in particular directions—though always with the exception that the purely retributive value of any sentence necessarily lies outside the field of scientific inquiry; for all the science in the world cannot measure whether a man has been punished as much as, or more or less than, he deserves. Nor can science assess the appropriate "denunciatory" value of a sentence. But, Lord Denning notwithstanding, this may perhaps be ignored, on the ground, as Professor Hart has put it, that "the idea that we may punish offenders against a moral code, not to prevent harm or suffering or even the repetition of the offence but simply as a means of venting or emphatically expressing moral condemnation, is uncomfortably close to human sacrifice as an expression of religious worship."[5]

On the assumption, however, that the primary function of the criminal courts is to discourage crime, theoretical goals can be formulated in terms which, though imprecise, are at least mutually consistent. Under such a preventive system I would myself say that the object of a sentence should be to take *the minimum action which offers an adequate prospect of preventing future offences*. Admittedly, in this formula imprecision lurks in the word "minimum," and this word implies also a moral judgment— the judgment, that is to say, that freedom to live one's life after the fashion of one's choice is of value in itself, and that even in the case of offenders any restriction of this freedom must always be weighted against the possible social damage which might result from further offences. Indeed, without this qualification my formula might be read as an invitation to capital punishment for everything from murder to illegal parking as the one certain method

[5] Hart, H. A. L., *Law, Liberty and Morality* (O.U.P., 1963), pp. 65, 66.

of preventing an offender from offending again. Nor again can any exact valuation be assigned to the word "adequate." In practice, the adequacy of any safeguard against further offences must be related to the gravity of the social damage which would result should such a recurrence in fact occur. In other words, it is proper to take risks with a petty thief which would be wholly unjustifiable in the case of a murderer.

This may suggest that in practice there is little difference between a professedly preventive system of sentencing and one designed to give an offender what he deserves. Both would normally give long sentences for grave crimes and light ones for minor offences. Up to a point this may well be so. But it is by no means clear that it would still be true if we had more reliable information as to the probable consequences of our decisions. Indeed, even as things are, in a situation in which we must rely almost wholly on hunches, I have found it a salutary exercise, when taking part in, or listening to, sentence decisions, to record privately against the sentence which is actually imposed that which I myself would have chosen in the light of my own hunches, had the discouragement of future offences been the primary objective. The two rarely coincide and the discrepancies are often substantial; but such an experiment has, of course, only a personal value if it is practised merely by one individual, all of whose hunches may well be wrong. If practised over a considerable period by a whole Bench[6] the results could be much more illuminating; and they would become more illuminating still as knowledge of the likely effects of future sentences becomes more securely founded.

The discouragement of future offences is, of course, itself a two-sided objective, involving as it must, calculations of the risk of future offences on the part of, on the

[6] "Sentencing exercises" have become common practice in conferences both of magistrates and of judges since the above words were written; and they continue to show up considerable discrepancies between one person's judgment and another's.

one hand, the person sentenced, and on the other hand, others who might be tempted to copy his regrettable example; nor can science determine the relative weight to be given to each of these alternatives, although each by itself is susceptible to scientific investigation. In practice, however, it is doubtless chiefly in the case of those offenders in whom any lively conscience is lacking—as in many professional criminals, motorists and youthful thieves—that the effect of sentences upon the community at large will call for special attention. For at the best of times, the sentence of the court must be regarded as a second-best substitute for the pangs of conscience or the superego. The sense of guilt, as I suggested in a previous lecture, is surely the most powerful of all deterrents. Apart from anything else, the pangs of a guilty conscience are an inevitable consequence of the commission of any crime to which they attach themselves: unlike the penalties prescribed by the law, they are not contingent upon the offence being detected.

The deterrent effects of sentences upon potential, as distinct from actual, offenders are, however, highly elusive, and at once more complex and more difficult to measure than is, I think, always appreciated. For, in the first place, if any such effects are to be realised at all, there must be some kind of rational, even if crude and semi-conscious, calculation on the part of the would-be offender: yet many crimes (and this certainly includes some of the most serious) are committed on an impulse that overrides any consideration whatsoever of their likely consequences. Secondly, the prospective offender must have a reasonably clear idea of the sentence that he is likely to incur, should the contemplated crime be detected. How accurate such forecasts actually are is a matter which might well be explored by survey techniques. That they can be very near the mark seems improbable, if only because sentences are known to vary very widely in accordance with the personal prejudices of those who impose them. In the case of the higher courts, discrepancies may indeed be kept within

bounds by the decisions of the Court of Appeal:
but in the case of magistrates' courts, from which appeal
lies normally to the Crown Court, no comparable unifying
influence is at work. As *The Times*[7] puts it, "Magistrates
have for centuries been effectively guided and controlled
by the High Court in most other matters. But no control
whatever can be exercised over them from the Strand in
matters of sentencing which are wholly within their own
discretion." If the chance of imprisonment for roughly
similar offences varies, as Roger Hood's figures,[8] quoted in
Chapter 1, show, from under 15 per cent. to around 50 per
cent., even the most sophisticated prospective criminal can
make but a crude guess at his chances; and in any case
what matters is not the sentence that he will actually get,
but what he thinks he will get; and as to the relation
between that subjective forecast and the sentence which is
objectively probable, we have absolutely no clue at all.
Every prospective offender calculating his prospects is like
a man trying to hit a moving object with a wobbling hand:
and everybody's wobbles are peculiar to himself.

Again, the risk of detection, which is often said to be the
vital factor in general deterrence, involves its own complexities. Since the end of the War the clear-up rate for
offences recorded by the police has generally fluctuated
between 40 per cent. and 45 per cent. - but "cleared up"
does not necessarily mean that the perpetrator has been
brought to book. Moreover, in estimating the deterrent
value of sentences we must once again distinguish between
objective and subjective calculations of the risks involved,
for it is the latter alone—the chances as seen by the
offender himself—which are likely to influence his
behaviour; and the relation of the subjective to the
objective risk will again vary according to individual
temperament. In the case of timid persons like myself, the
subjective estimate is likely always to exceed the objective

7 *The Times*, October 20, 1962.
8 See p. 13, above.

reality: such persons are always convinced that their offences will be detected even in circumstances in which this is in fact quite unlikely. Bolder spirits, on the other hand, are likely to err on the other side; whilst in moments of extreme passion the validity of anyone's subjective forecast may well be reduced to zero. Finally the anticipated penalty must be weighted against the prospective returns (again as subjectively estimated) from the crime. It may be worth running a big risk for a big reward but not for a smaller one.

That calculations of this kind are sometimes made seems pretty clear. They may well be made on the grand scale by professional criminals, and they are certainly often present, in more modest terms, to the minds of many motorists. It can, for instance, hardly be doubted that the streets of our cities would be cleared, if the normal penalty for parking in a prohibited place was a year's imprisonment and disqualification from driving for life. But even in that event, if the chances of detection were known to be fairly low, and if a brief period of illegal parking might result in a million-pound deal, there would be some who would rate the risk worth taking. Nor is the impact of "exemplary sentences"—such as those imposed on the Notting Hill race rioters some years ago—by any means necessarily as dramatic as is sometimes assumed. After those sentences, the riots did indeed die down; but who knows how far this was due to the severity of the sentences themselves or to the public disgust which the riots provoked? And in so far as credit is due to the sentences, how long will they be remembered and therefore retain their effectiveness? Since the Notting Hill episode, sporadic outbreaks of similar racial violence have occurred in other parts of the country which also have quickly faded out. How did the sentences in these cases compare with those imposed on the Notting Hill rioters, and have any differences been correlated with the subsequent history of race riots in different districts? All these questions have to be answered before we can even begin to assess the effectiveness of deterrence upon the public at large.

The Home Office is, I understand, already involved in research on the subject of general deterrence; but in the meantime the facts have to be faced, first, that in concrete terms we are almost totally ignorant of the deterrent effect on potential offenders attributable to particular sentences; and, secondly, that in any case the influences which prevent members of the public at large from committing crimes are extremely complex, and that the prospect of what will befall them if they should offend is only one, and often quite a minor one, amongst such influences.

For this reason, it would seem sensible, on purely practical grounds, normally to give priority (though not necessarily always exclusive consideration) in the choice of sentence, to the likely effect of a particular decision upon the offender himself. If we have practically no idea as to how to achieve one of our two objectives, common sense would suggest that we should concentrate upon the other, in which the prospects of success are, at the least, a little brighter. Such concentration, moreover, has the incidental advantage that it offers the best—indeed I would say the only—hope of eliminating the influence of personal prejudices upon sentences. Most magistrates would, I think, agree that it is psychologically almost impossible to emancipate oneself from one's personal assessment of the wickedness of particular acts or particular offenders; and most of us have a special abhorrence of certain crimes— whether homosexuality, or reckless motoring or stealing from one's employer. Since, moreover, these prejudices vary greatly from individual to individual, they almost inevitably result in gross discrepancies between sentences for which no justification can be found. Many experiments have been made which illustrate the potential magnitude of these discrepancies. Mr. E. S. Gonning, for instance, the Honorary Secretary of the Essex branch of the Magistrates' Association, has described the range of penalties suggested in a meeting of both magistrates and general public for certain imaginary cases. On the average the sentences suggested by both magistrates and non-magistrates ran pretty close to one another: but these averages concealed wide individual differences ranging, for example, in a given case from conditional discharge up to anything between one and twelve months' imprisonment[9]; and similar discrepancies have resulted when magistrates have been asked to assess the fines appropriate in typical motoring cases. Moreover, even if a rough agreement can be obtained as to the "tariff" to be observed, no objective test exists whereby the correctness of the tariff itself can be demonstrated.

Assessments of guilt are, and must remain, purely subjective; and we can all cling to our own opinions secure in the knowledge that no one can prove us wrong. By contrast, the frequency with which reconviction follows a sentence for a given offence is a fact. If the purpose of a sentence is to reduce this frequency, an objective criterion immediately becomes available by which the merits of the courts' policy can be estimated. In course of time, as evidence of the results of sentencing policy accumulates, all of us can be proved right or wrong; and the more passionate our personal detestation of any particular crime, the more eager should we be to follow the course which is demonstrably most likely to prevent its recurrence.

What practical steps, then, can be taken to develop the prevalent punitive system of sentencing into one the success of which is judged by its skill in preventing recidivism? Obviously here the first requisite is better information as to the results of court decisions—notably in the form of more numerous and more ambitious prediction studies. Hitherto, however, in most of the studies that are so described, "predictive" has been merely a courtesy title; for these investigations are more inclined to tell us what we might have done in the past rather than

[9] *The Magistrate* (1963), Vol. XIX, No. 4.

what we should now do for the future. Yet even so, mastery of the lessons of the past is the first step towards future wisdom, as has been shown in this country both by the Mannheim and Wilkins investigation into the risks of recidivism in Borstal inmates,[10] and in the Home Office Research Unit's study of Persistent Criminals[11]—in both of which statistical analysis proved to have a higher prognostic value than the subjective judgments of persons such as prison officers who were in close touch with the subjects of the investigation. Moreover, even if researches of this kind have scarcely yet reached the stage at which they can give much practical guidance to a court engaged in the actual task of sentencing, they may well be used to improve the power of discrimination as to the quality of the information supplied to the courts.

As the Streatfeild Committee pointed out,[12] such information is steadily increasing in volume, although existing arrangements have developed sporadically and piecemeal—and, it might be added, without much regard to the relevance of the material supplied to the purposes for which it is required. Certainly it is a common experience of those who have to decide on sentences that the task *seems* much easier if they are provided with fairly full biographies of the offenders concerned. A good social history, it has been said, makes the Bench feel cosy: but does it result in a better sentence? Here the Home Office Research Unit's analysis of the information used by the Preventive Detention Advisory Board[13] in the allocation of prisoners to third stage is illuminating. In spite of a very close correlation between the Board's allocation and most

[10]Mannheim, H. and Wilkins, L.T., *Prediction Methods in Relation to Borstal Training* (H.M.S.O., 1955).

[11]Hammond. W. H. and Chayen, E., *Persistent Criminals* (H.M.S.O., 1963).

[12] Interdepartmental Committee on the Business of the Criminal Courts, *Report* (H.M.S.O., 1961), Cmnd. 1289, paras. 264 *et seq.*

[13]Preventive detention having now been abolished, this Board no longer exists.

of the information given them by the prison, the selection was not successful in distinguishing those who were later reconvicted; and further analysis showed that very few of the numerous items of information collected had much bearing on the likelihood of reconvictions. Altogether, the authors of this report conclude, it is doubtful whether in its present form the information supplied to the Board can be much help in selecting the offenders least likely to be reconvicted. Yet, if this conclusion appears depressingly negative, it is encouraging to find that the investigators themselves were able to show that the few items in the offenders' backgrounds which were related to reconviction could in fact be combined in such a way as to differentiate groups with very different reconviction rates—ranging from 59 per cent. in the most hopeful to 92 per cent. in the most vulnerable group.[14]

Hitherto, moreover, the practical usefulness of prediction studies has been restricted by the fact that they have concerned themselves chiefly with the comparative vulnerability to reconviction of different offenders upon whom the same sentence has been passed; whereas the task of the courts is to choose between different sentences which may be imposed upon the same types of offender. The techniques involved in exploration of this problem would not, however, seem to be much more complicated than those already in use; and their application to the problem of differential sentencing might, moreover, throw some light upon the curious and depressing uniformity of the consequences of various types of sentence—as illustrated by Sir George Benson's and Leslie Wilkins' investigations mentioned earlier in this lecture. As Wilkins has said, it is clear that "there is no generally good treatment—that is to say, one which is suited for all types of case. It seems that it is necessary to examine the interplay between offenders and treatment, rather than to consider treatment as a single

[14] Hammond and Chayen, *op. cit.*, pp. 142-147.

variable. The 'treatment' indicated for different types of offenders may be contra-indicated for others."[15]

Certain American experiments have indeed already succeeded in showing differential effects of the same treatment upon different types of offender. In one Naval Correctional Station, for example, it has been found that subjects classed as socially immature improved under a spell of more or less conventional discipline, but were actually made worse by exposure to intensive psychotherapy, although this latter type of treatment apparently had good results on offenders classed as having greater social maturity. Similar results, too, have been reported from the California Board of Corrections,[16] in an experiment in which some 400 older juvenile offenders were divided into two classes designated as amenable or not amenable to treatment by intensive counselling. Half of each class was then subjected to such treatment, with the result that amongst the amenables those who were treated did better than those who were not; whereas in the non-amenable group the subsequent record of the treated was actually worse than that of the untreated.

Limited as is the scope of these researches, they are already promising enough to raise the question of how much longer sentencing can continue to be conducted by the present amateurish, hit-and-miss methods. They certainly strengthen the case for some training in penology being required of those upon whom the duty of deciding sentences devolves. Yet as long ago as 1925 the Ninth International Prison Congress resolved at its meeting in London that "judicial studies should be supplemented by criminological ones." In the view of that Congress,

"The study of criminal psychology and sociology,

[15] Wilkins, L. T., "Crime, Cause and Treatment: Recent Research Theory," *Educational Research* (1961), Vol. IV, No. 1.

[16] Adams, Stuart, *Interaction between Individual Interview Therapy and Treatment Amenability in Older Youth Authority Wards* (State of California Board of Corrections Monograph No. 2, 1961).

forensic medicine and psychiatry, and penology
should be obligatory for all who wish to judge in
criminal cases. Such judges . . . should have a full
knowledge of prisons and similar institutions and
should visit them frequently."[17]

Indeed, even earlier still, in 1905, a meeting convened by
the French group of the International Union of Criminal
Law had unanimously recommended that "there should be
organised in the faculties of law special teaching, theoretical
and practical, for the whole range of penal studies," and
that "the certificate in penal studies awarded should be
taken into consideration for nomination to and advancement in the magistracy."[18] Nevertheless, in this country,
although lay magistrates are already required to take
courses of instruction which include some discussion of
penological subjects, no comparable studies have any place
in the normal training of the judiciary, which retains its
purely legal character. Indeed in reply to a parliamentary
question[19] as to the steps taken to bring the Home Office
Research Unit's publication *Persistent Criminals* to the
attention of those responsible for sentencing offenders, the
Minister of State, Home Office, made the remarkable statement that "it is not the general practice to take special
steps to bring publications of this nature to the notice of
the courts," and in answer to a supplementary question he
added that "one should bear in mind here the highly
technical nature of this particular Report. It was felt, in
view of that, that it was hardly caviare for the general—
even for the court." Asked whether this implied that those
who have to pass sentences are not capable of understanding this Report, the Minister disclaimed any such

[17] Butler, A. W., "Ninth International Prison Congress," *Journal of
the American Institute of Criminal Law and Criminology* (1925/26),
Vol. 16, p. 605.

[18] Radzinowicz, L., *In Search of Criminology* (Heinemann, 1961),
p. 70.

[19] House of Lords Official Report, May 27, 1963, cols. 554-555.

admission; yet this would certainly seem to be the obvious inference. And what indeed is the purpose of these researches, if they are not to be brought to the attention of, or are not intelligible to, those who could make use of their findings?

At the same time hints of change are in the wind. The Streatfeild Committee [20] recommended the publication of a booklet covering all forms of sentence and written specially for sentencers "as a first step towards a textbook on sentencing," and this recommendation has been accepted by the government. Moreover, the Committee went so far as to say that "Sentencing is, in a sense, an emergent branch of the law, and it may be expected that, as in other branches of the law, the accumulated know-ledge and experience will eventually reach a stage of development when a separate textbook is required"; and they added the observation that "in our view a sentencer can more fully grasp what sentences involve by visiting penal institutions than by reading a factual summary, how-ever comprehensive." There would seem to be a broad enough hint here; but to have gone further would no doubt have involved transgressing the limits of the Committee's terms of reference.

The Streatfeild Report included also the potentially important recommendation [21] that a sentencer should be able to obtain from a central authority follow-up information about any case in which he has a particular interest. It is much to be hoped that free use will be made of this, for it will enable persons passing sentence to check their own forecasts against the subsequent facts, and so to rate their own performance. Even before it becomes possible to base sentences upon generalised predictions which have a reasonably solid scientific foundation, it is pretty certain that some people's hunches will turn out to

[20] Interdepartmental Committee on the Business of the Criminal Courts, *Report* (H.M.S.O., 1961), Cmnd. 1289, paras. 299-302.

[21] *Ibid.* para. 305.

be better than others—just as in interviewing, even when no one is able to say confidently exactly what are the favourable or unfavourable signs to look for in an interviewee, some interviewers prove to be consistently better than others at spotting the type of man they want. In a more ruthless world, perhaps, those whose performance at sentencing proved to be consistently unsuccessful might be diverted to other occupations; but even apart from this, it would be highly illuminating for those who are engaged in the business at least to be able to check on the validity of their own judgments, and so perhaps to use experience in such a way as to improve future performance. I can only repeat the hope that, at no matter what cost in pestering the Home Office, we shall all make the fullest use of this new opportunity.

Any requirement of more formal training in this country, however, may run into the difficulty that English judges are not trained as such. In contrast with the Continental system, under which those who seek judicial office follow a different course throughout their careers from that pursued by those who do not, English judges, recorders, circuit judges and professional magistrates are appointed, without reference to specific additional qualifications from among practising barristers (or in certain cases also from among those who have practised as solicitors). Yet even so, if a substantial place could be found for penological subjects as an option in the Bar examinations, it would at least be possible in making these appointments to give some credit to those who held a penological qualification.

Already both in Canada and in the United States more attention seems to be paid to sentencing policy than is yet the case here. In the United States, Congress passed a law in 1958 authorising the creation of Sentencing Institutes, "In the interest of uniformity of sentencing procedures," and with a view to "the formulation of sentencing principles and criteria to assist in promoting the equitable administration of the criminal laws of the United States."

Accordingly meetings of federal judges have been organised for discussion both of general problems and of the actual sentences that each individual judge would propose in sample cases; and in Canada seminars are being held from time to time on similar lines. At the present stage the discussions in these meetings, which appear to range very widely, seem to be chiefly concerned with the search for a common philosophy and common principles of sentencing, and with the elimination of wide disparities for which no rational justification can be found—in other words with the establishment of a common tariff. Study of empirical evidence as to the effects of particular sentences is less in evidence. But the trend is significant.

All these developments are designed to improve the efficiency of the various judicial authorities to whom it now falls to pass sentences. An alternative course, favoured by Professor Nigel Walker, is to take the job away from them altogether and give it to somebody else. Walker criticises the Streatfeild proposals[22] on the ground that they are an attempt to "patch up a system which is really wasting the time of highly trained and highly paid judges to no good purpose." The Committee, he says, "proposed not only that we should continue to waste the time of people trained to try questions of guilt or innocence by asking them to make decisions of another kind, but also that we should now expect them to spend a lot of their spare time studying penal statistics." Besides, he suggests, far too many people now have a hand in the job. If we really want to get trained and efficient sentencers, the way to do it is to reduce to the minimum the number of people who have to be kept informed and trained, and to keep them in close touch with one another and with those who provide them with their information.

Such a proposal means in effect that decisions as to the treatment of offenders should become an administrative,

[22] Walker, Nigel, "The Sentence of the Court," *The Listener*, June 28, 1962.

instead of a judicial, matter—though Professor Walker would leave with the courts in the first instance the choice between a custodial sentence and one which did not involve loss of liberty. Given, however, that some kind of detention was thought to be necessary, it would, under his scheme, be for the executive authorities and not for the courts to decide both upon its duration (perhaps within a prescribed maximum) and upon its nature. Indeed it is one of the chief merits of this proposal that the exercise of some such executive power alone makes indeterminate sentences possible: for the court which passes such a sentence must leave to those who take control of the prisoner the decision as to when he may safely be released.

I have already argued in a previous lecture that custodial sentences should be indeterminate in respect of the type of institution to which an offender should be committed, and indeed that the rigid division of institutions into the medical and the penal should be obliterated; and the arguments in favour of indeterminacy in duration are in principle similar. If the primary object of a sentence is to discourage further offences at the cost of minimal interference with liberty, then the moment at which this discouragement is effective enough to justify the offender's release can hardly be forecast in advance: it must depend upon his progress. Logically, therefore, the conception of criminal procedure as preventive rather than punitive involves acceptance of indeterminate sentences.

Hitherto, however, such indeterminacy has not been popular in this country though it is widely used abroad. The chief arguments that are used against it seem to be, on the one hand, that offenders do not like it, and, on the other hand, that it is unpopular also with the prison authorities. One need not, perhaps, pay too much attention to the first of these arguments, though I must myself confess to having once been swayed by the pleas of a youth for whom the court was proposing a Borstal sentence that we should substitute six months in a detention centre so as to guarantee his release by the time that his girlfriend expected their baby to be born. As to the second argument, this seems to carry less weight than it did; for, whatever the theoretical objections, indeterminacy is in fact rapidly creeping into our practice. In particular it is now the rule, not only for life sentences, but also for those offenders under 21 for whom six months is thought to be too little and three years too long a period of detention. Under the Criminal Justice Act of 1961[23] prison sentences between these limits may no longer be imposed on persons of age to qualify for a Borstal sentence. An indeterminate Borstal sentence thus becomes the only form of detention permissible for this category.

All the same, indeterminacy does, I think, demand safeguards; and I would whole-heartedly support both Professor Walker and the late Sir Rupert Cross[24] in proposing to leave with the courts, at any rate for the time being, the power to fix a maximum period of detention. In the present state of knowledge decisions as to release are bound to be very much hit-and-miss affairs. Mistakes will be made, and the temptation to play for safety will be strong; and it is a temptation that besets the psychiatric quite as much as other custodians, and is not less strong in that its appeal is to the best of motives. Both the white-coated and the blue-coated jailer alike need protection against it, just as we in our turn need protection against their virtuous zeal; and it is still to the courts that we must look to preserve the principle of minimal interference.

To this I myself would add a second safeguard which Walker thinks unnecessary—namely that decisions as to detention or release should not be left to an "invisible

---

[23] This provision has since been repealed, and it is now (1980) proposed that a uniform system of residential institutions for young adult offenders should replace the present division into prisons and Borstal training institutions.

[24] Cross, R., "Indeterminate Sentences," *The Listener*, February 15, 1962.

office," but should only be made by those who have some face-to-face contact with the person concerned. In saying this I do not forget that some of the best predictions of the risk of recidivism have been made without any first-hand contact with their subjects, and that the stage may well some day be reached when this risk will be estimated by computers who must be presumed to be quite unmoved by personal contacts. Indeed I understand that Professor W. T. Williams at the University of Southampton is already engaged, with the co-operation of a computer known as Pegasus, in research along these lines. But complete objectivity is a long way off yet. Until these predictors are demonstrably more reliable than they are today, so that the objectively best decision becomes self-evident, there is a real risk that paper decisions will be made on a routine basis in accordance with standardised rules which in particular instances may be very wide indeed of the mark. Those who have had experience in the past of the Home Office allocation of children to approved schools by officers whose first-hand knowledge of the child is nil, and of the schools not apparently much greater, may appreciate the force of this danger, as complaints about our parole system testify.[25] No one believes in the justice of an invisible office.

To this sketch of the main implications of a sentencing policy aimed primarily at the prevention of crime, two postscripts must now be added. First, the suggestion that sentencing is becoming an increasingly expert business for which its practitioners should be suitably trained does not mean that it should be handed over to psychiatrists. Fundamentally, the job is statistical not psychiatric: it is a question of detecting on the one hand those factors in the offender's personality and circumstances and in the particular crime which he has committed which are correlated with his probable subsequent behaviour; and on the other hand those which indicate the treatment to

[25] See Postscript to Chapter 2, pp. 62 *et seq.*

which he is most likely to make a satisfactory response. In the second of these fields a psychiatrist should be able to pronounce upon the outlook for medical treatment of one sort or another; and on the first his specialised experience may make him able to make better guesses than most laymen. But the business of marshalling the multiple factors in past experience in such a way as to illuminate future probabilities is not in itself a psychological process; and it is not without significance that the purely statistical Mannheim and Wilkins predictions proved better than those of the professional psychologists.[26]

Secondly, a sentencing policy which makes the prevention of crime its primary objective is not necessarily to be equated with one that is "soft." Such a policy is non-punitive in the sense that it neither regards punishment as an end in itself nor evaluates crimes and those who commit them in terms of what each is thought to deserve. But, while adhering to the principle of minimum action, it does not rule out the use of penalties or discard deterrence altogether. For everyone knows that human beings respond to a variety of stimuli; and that the responses vary both as between one individual and another and in the same individual in different circumstances. One man may make rich use of opportunity where another may be shocked into change only by the loss of cherished privileges. One responds to psychotherapy, another to strict discipline, while for a third perhaps the only hope is an extremely liberal and rewarding regime. *Quot homines tot*—in a new sense—*sententiae.*

That the criminal courts should unashamedly aim at the reduction of criminal behaviour, and that regard should be paid to questions of guilt and responsibility only in so far as they are related to this aim, will no doubt be regarded by some as monstrous, and by others as Utopian. Those who hold the first of these views may perceive a threat to

[26]Mannheim, H. and Wilkins, L.T., *Prediction Methods in Relation to Borstal Training* (H.M.S.O., 1955), p. 141.

traditional ideas of justice; and in this, it must be admitted, there may be some force, since current conceptions of justice in sentencing are closely related to the idea of a sentence tariff—to the principle that a sentence should be primarily related to the gravity of the offence and to the measure of the offender's guilt, rather than to its probable future consequences. To this the only possible reply is that the blind figure holding the even scales is not necessarily the appropriate image for a civilised society, and that it might be a mark of maturity to discard this in favour of the justice which would deal open-eyed with each according to his need rather than according to his deserts. Any suggestion, however, that such maturity has anywhere yet been generally attained may equally well be dismissed as Utopian; and, since the courts cannot afford to be too far ahead of public opinion, the approach to this goal must in practice necessarily be gradual. That is why even those of us who are most anxious to travel this way never wholly practise what we preach.

But what, I think, cannot be denied is that at the very least the choice between alternatives is becoming steadily sharper. With growing recognition of the heterogeneity of crimes, and of the persons by whom and the circumstances in which they are committed, it must become increasingly plain that individual responses to penal treatments are no less heterogeneous, and that like sentences will constantly provoke quite unlike results. At the same time the proliferation of offences of strict liability on the one hand and the continual refinement of notions of responsibility on the other have between them muddied the notion of a crime as the product of a guilty mind to a degree which threatens to obliterate the traditional, punitive concept of the courts' function. And most important of all, as predictions become more reliable, and more readily applicable to actual cases, the refuge of ignorance becomes less and less reliable, and the pretence that sentencing by deserts is society's best protection becomes less and less tenable. Today the future consequences of any given sentence can be estimated only to such a low degree of probability that there is every excuse for ignoring them. But suppose that probability to be raised much higher—then the choice will have to be faced—which do we want to do?—to punish the wicked as they deserve or to diminish crime? Would any of us then have the courage to impose sentences which, though just enough by traditional standards, we knew to be likely to encourage, rather than to prevent, recidivism? That, I suggest, will be the challenge of a by no means distant future.

POSTSCRIPT TO CHAPTER 4

This lecture calls for relatively little amendment or comment since it is in the main an exposition of my personal view of what should be the objective of sentencing - and that has not changed materially over the years. The lecture should however, be read against Nigel Walker's admirable recent book[1] in which he classifies sentencing policies as "Punishing, denouncing or reducing" (with some subsequent finer sub-divisions). In this categorisation I myself rank as a "reductionist." I would, however, claim that the ultimate aim of all three schools is reductivist, inasmuch as adherents of all of them wish to see the volume of crime reduced. Certainly it is hard to imagine that a "punitive" sentencer whose primary purpose is to punish an offender as he deserves would go so far as to impose a punishment which he had reason to believe would make either the person subject to it, or other people more rather than less likely to commit similar crimes in future; and the same is true of the denunciator, who in the first instance regards a sentence as a symbolic demonstration both to the person concerned and to the public at large of the iniquity of the crime for which it is imposed. However, be that as it may, I would strongly recommend Walker's book as a complement (or corrective?) to my lectures.

Perhaps the saddest feature of the 17 years that have elapsed since these lectures were delivered is that, in spite of all the words that have been spoken and books and papers that have been written on penal policy, the crime rate has persistently risen; nor has there been any improvement in the clear-up rate of offences recorded by the police. Indeed the clear-up rate in 1978 is actually lower

---

[1] Walker, Professor Nigel, *Punishment, Danger and Stigma* (Blackwell, 1980).

than it was in 1961. Moreover the prisons are more crowded than ever.

And still we keep on trying to do better. In due course a Home office pamphlet on *The Sentence of the Court* was produced, as recommended by the Streatfeild Committee, and is now circulated to all magistrates. Its 1964 edition included the results of an extensive follow-up of a number of offenders involved in similar crimes, which found that first-time burglars responded better to probation than did thieves, upon whom fines apparently had more effect. But how much does that sort of discovery help? It certainly does not indicate that all burglars should be put on probation and all thieves fined for their first offence. But on rare occasions, when a court has been hesitating whether to fine a burglar or thief or to put him on probation, recollection of this finding has floated into my mind and just tipped the scale. However, the practical usefulness of such researches will not be increased unless and until magistrates are more disposed to study statistical investigation, than in my experience they as yet appear to be. This particular Appendix soon disappeared from later editions of the pamphlet.

Equally depressing is the Home Office Research Unit's Report on *Residential Treatment and its Effects on Delinquency*[2] which spent five chapters on producing evidence to show that residential programmes are "largely ineffective in reducing the incidence of delinquent behaviour," and then added two others in an attempt to explain this failure and to suggest remedies. Similarly the statistics of recidivism amongst ex-prisoners go from bad to worse: the proportion of male offenders reconvicted within two years of discharge from prisons, detention centres or borstals has risen from 52 per cent. in 1971 to 58 per cent. in 1976, while the corresponding figures for females are 33 per cent. in 1971 and 43 per cent. in 1976. Indeed the

---

[2] *Residential Treatment and its Effects on Delinquency*, Home Office Research Study No. 32 (July 1975).

concept of imprisonment as a reformative experience is so unrealistic that one of the criticisms not unfairly levelled against the Parole Board's prediction table is that the most reliable source of data as to an offender's probable career after imprisonment is to be found in his pre-imprisonment history.

Clearly, in the light of the information at present available sentencing policy is, by reductivist standards, far from successful. Unhappily also the promised opportunity for individual sentencers to have access to the subsequent history of their own cases has remained a dead letter; and there remains one regrettable gap in the information generally available, to which I have already referred in the Postscript to Chapter 2 - namely the lack of any comprehensive statistics, analogous to those relating to persons discharged from custodial institutions, which would record the subsequent recidivism of offenders who have completed sentences under Community Service Orders. Now that these Orders are imposed at the rate of about 13,000 a year the time is surely ripe for an investigation to be undertaken which would compare the records of ex-community service workers with those of ex-prisoners in similar cases.

My final lecture ended on a relatively optimistic note, still cherishing the hope (expressed in my first lecture, pages 16 *et seq*.) that more refined methods of investigation, together with the rapid growth of electronic mechanisms for handling more complex data, may make sentencers better aware of the results of their own decisions, and more competent to achieve whatever it is that they want to achieve. But I have to confess that over the years since these lectures were delivered, I have been increasingly haunted by the image suggested in the concluding paragraph of my first lecture of the whole penal system as in a sense a gigantic irrelevance - wholly misconceived as a method of controlling phenomena the origins of which are inextricably rooted in the structure of our society.